THE NORTH YORK MOORS

50 WALKS IN THE NATIONAL PARK

by Paddy Dillon

JUNIPER HOUSE, MURLEY MOSS,
OXENHOLME ROAD, KENDAL, CUMBRIA LA9 7RL
www.cicerone.co.uk

© Paddy Dillon 2019
Second edition 2019
ISBN: 978 1 85284 951 1
First edition 2005

Printed by KHL Printing, Singapore
A catalogue record for this book is available from the British Library.

Updates to this Guide

While every effort is made by our authors to ensure the accuracy of guidebooks as they go to print, changes can occur during the lifetime of an edition. Any updates that we know of for this guide will be on the Cicerone website (www.cicerone.co.uk/951/updates), so please check before planning your trip. We also advise that you check information about such things as transport, accommodation and shops locally. Even rights of way can be altered over time. We are always grateful for information about any discrepancies between a guidebook and the facts on the ground, sent by email to updates@cicerone.co.uk or by post to Cicerone, Juniper House, Murley Moss, Oxenholme Road, Kendal, LA9 7RL.

Register your book: To sign up to receive free updates, special offers and GPX files where available, register your book at www.cicerone.co.uk.

Front cover: Looking across Bilsdale from high on Rievaulx Moor (Walk 8)

THE NORTH YORK MOORS

About the Author

Paddy Dillon is a prolific walker and guidebook writer, with over 90 guidebooks to his name and contributions to 40 other titles. He has written extensively for many different outdoor publications and has appeared on radio and television.

Paddy uses a tablet computer to write his route descriptions while walking. His descriptions are therefore precise, having been written at the very point at which the reader uses them.

Paddy is an indefatigable long-distance walker who has walked all of Britain's National Trails and several major European trails. He lives on the fringes of the Lake District and has walked, and written about walking, in every county throughout the British Isles. He has led guided walks and walked throughout Europe, as well as in Nepal, Tibet, Korea, Africa and the Rocky Mountains of Canada and the US. Paddy is a member of the Outdoor Writers and Photographers Guild and President of the Backpackers Club.

Other Cicerone guides by the author

Glyndwr's Way
Mountain Walking in Mallorca
The Cleveland Way and the Yorkshire Wolds Way
The GR20 Corsica
The GR5 Trail
The Great Glen Way
The Irish Coast to Coast Walk
The Mountains of Ireland
The National Trails
The North York Moors
The Pennine Waye Reivers Way
The South West Coast Path
The Teesdale Way
The Wales Coast Path
Trekking in Greenland
Trekking in Mallorca
Trekking in the Alps

Walking and Trekking in Iceland
Walking in County Durham
Walking on Madeira
Walking in Menorca
Walking in Sardinia
Walking in the Isles of Scilly
Walking in the North Pennines
Walking on Arran
Walking on Gran Canaria
Walking on Guernsey
Walking on Jersey
Walking on La Gomera and El Hierro
Walking on La Palma
Walking on Lanzarote and Fuerteventura
Walking on Malta
Walking on Tenerife
Walking the Galloway Hills

CONTENTS

Route symbols on OS map extracts

 route

 alternative route

 link route/detour

 start/finish point

 start point

 finish point

 route direction

for OS legend see printed OS maps

GPX files
for all routes can be downloaded free at
www.cicerone.co.uk/951/GPX

Overview map

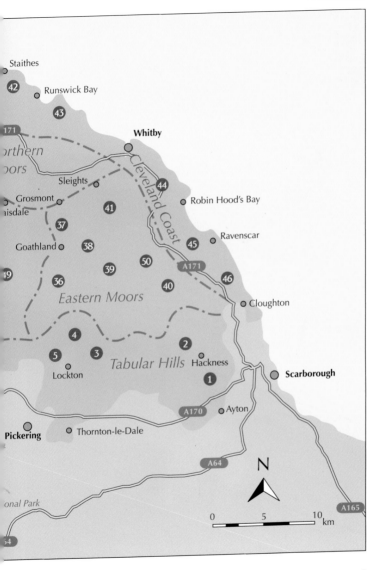

Sheep grazing has ensured that the dales have been close cropped for centuries

INTRODUCTION

This guidebook offers 50 walks in the varied landscape of the North York Moors National Park. The park was designated in 1952 and covers 1432km^2 (553 square miles) of land, comprising the largest continuous expanse of heather moorland in England. The moors are of no great height yet offer a wonderful sense of spaciousness, with extensive views under a 'big sky'. There are also deep verdant dales where charming scenes and hoary stone buildings can be found, as well as a remarkable cliff coastline designated as the North Yorkshire and Cleveland Heritage Coast. The long-distance Cleveland Way wraps itself around the moors and coast, but there are many other walks that explore the rich variety of the area, focusing on its charm, history, heritage and wildlife.

The walks are distributed through seven regions within the park, enabling walkers to discover and appreciate the Tabular Hills, Hambleton Hills, Cleveland Hills, Northern Moors, High Moors, Eastern Moors and Cleveland Coast. For those who like a challenge, the course of the classic Lyke Wake Walk, crossing the national park from east to west, is also offered, split over a four-day period to allow a leisurely appreciation of the moors. Almost 725km (450 miles) of walking routes are described here, although the national park could furnish you with many more splendid ones from a stock of 1770km (1100 miles) of public footpaths and bridleways.

People have crossed the North York Moors since time immemorial, and some of their routes survive to this day. Stout stone crosses were planted to assist travellers and traders with a safe passage, and these days practically all rights of way are signposted and walkable, although some routes are used far more than others.

Despite having the appearance of a wilderness, this area has often been, and remains to this day, a working landscape. The moors are scarred and quarried in places by man's search for mineral resources, and the heather cover requires year-round management for the sport of grouse shooting. Walkers with enquiring minds will quickly realise that the human history and settlement of the moors, even at its highest points, stretches back over thousands of years. Our own enjoyment of the moors, in contrast, may be nothing more than a transient pleasure.

BRIEF HISTORY OF THE MOORS

Early settlement

The first people to roam across the North York Moors were Mesolithic

Walkers follow an old railway trackbed above Rosedale (Walk 30)

nomads, eking out an existence as hunter-gatherers some 10,000 years ago. Swampy lowlands surrounded the uplands, and apart from a few flakes of flint these people left little trace of their existence. Evidence of the Neolithic settlers who followed can be seen in the mounds of stones they heaped over their burial sites, called barrows, which date back to 2000BC. Soon afterwards, from 1800BC onwards, the Beaker People and Bronze Age invaders moved into the area. They used more advanced methods of land clearance and tillage, and buried their dead in conspicuous mounds known as 'howes'. These people exhausted the land, clearing too much forest too quickly. Minerals leached from the thin soils, so that the uplands became unproductive. Climate changes led to ground becoming waterlogged and mossy, so that tillage became impossible and scrub moorland developed. Iron Age people faced more of a struggle to survive and had to organise themselves in defensive promontory forts. Perhaps some of the linear dykes that cut across the countryside date from that time, although many structures are difficult to date with any degree of certainty.

Roman settlement

The Romans marched through Britain during the first century and founded a city at York. Perhaps the most important site on the North York Moors was Cawthorn Camp near Cropton, which was used as a military training ground. Although Wade's Causeway in Wheeldale is often referred to as a Roman road, it may not be. Hadrian's

Wall kept the Picts at bay to the north, but the east coast was open to invasion by the Saxons, so the Romans built coastal signal stations in AD368 at Hartlepool, Hunt Cliff, Boulby, Goldsborough, Whitby, Ravenscar, Scarborough, Filey and Flamborough Head. Some of these sites have been lost as the cliffs have receded. By AD410 the Romans had left Britain, and the coast was clear for wave upon wave of invasions.

Dark Age settlement

Saxons, Angles, Danes and other invaders left their mark on the North York Moors, establishing little villages and tilling the land, mostly in the dales, as the higher ground had long since reverted to scrub. Many of these settlers were Christian, and in AD657 a monastery in the Celtic Christian tradition was founded at Whitby. Whitby Abbey was notable for one of its early lay brothers, Caedmon, who was inspired to sing, and whose words comprise the earliest written English Christian verse. During the successive waves of invasion there were times of strife, and the abbey was destroyed in AD867. Other small-scale rural monastic sites are known. Many early Christian churches were simple wooden buildings. Some of the earliest carved stone crosses date from the 10th century.

Norman settlement

A more comprehensive invasion was mounted by the Normans, who swept through the region during the 11th century. They totally reorganised society, establishing the feudal system and leaving an invaluable insight into the

Lilla Cross is the oldest Christian monument on the moors (Walk 40)

state of the countryside through the vast numbers of settlements and properties listed in the Domesday Book. In return for allegiance to the king, noblemen were handed vast tracts of countryside and authority over its inhabitants. Resentment and violence was rife for a time, and the new overlords were obliged to build robust castles. Many noblemen gifted large parts of their estates to religious orders from mainland Europe, encouraging them to settle in the area.

Monastic settlement

Monasteries and abbeys were founded in and around the North York Moors in the wake of the Norman invasion, and ruins dating from the 12th and 13th centuries still dominate the countryside. Stone quarrying was important at this time, and large-scale sheep rearing was developed, leading to the large, close-cropped pastures that feature in the dales. There were still plenty of woodlands for timber and hunting, but the moors remained bleak and barren and were reckoned to be of little worth. Early maps and descriptions by travellers dismissed the area as 'black-a-moor', yet it was necessary for people to cross the moors if only to get from place to place, and so a network of paths developed. The monasteries planted some of the old stone crosses on the moors to provide guidance to travellers. This era came to a sudden close with Henry VIII's dissolution of the monasteries in the 16th century.

Recent settlement

Over the past few centuries the settlement of the North York Moors has

Whitby and Whitby Abbey as seen from the Whalebone Arch (Walk 44)

been influenced by its mineral wealth and the burgeoning tourist industry. At the beginning of the 17th century an amazing chemical industry developed to extract highly prized alum from a particular type of of shale. This industry lasted two and a half centuries and had a huge impact around the cliff-bound fringes of the North York Moors. From the mid-18th to mid-19th centuries, Whitby's fishing industry specialised in whaling, and the town benefitted greatly. The 19th century was the peak period for jet production, often referred to as Whitby Jet. Railways were built in and around the North York Moors throughout the 19th century, bringing an increase in trade and allowing easier shipment of ironstone from the moors. Railways also laid the foundation for a brisk tourist trade, injecting new life into coastal resorts whose trade and fishing fleets were on the wane. Tourism continues to be one of the most important industries in the area, and tourism in the countryside is very much dependent on walking.

NORTH YORK MOORS INDUSTRIES

Alum

Throughout the North York Moors National Park huge piles of flaky pink shale have been dumped on the landscape, sometimes along the western fringes of the Cleveland Hills, but more especially along the coast. These are the remains of a large-scale chemical industry that thrived from 1600 to 1870. The hard-won prize was alum: a salt that could be extracted from certain beds of shale through a time-consuming process.

Wherever the shale occurred, it was extensively quarried. Millions of tons were cut, changing the shape of the landscape, especially along the coast. Wood, and in later years coal, was layered with the shale, and huge piles were set on fire and kept burning for months, sometimes even a whole year. The burnt shale was then soaked in huge tanks of water, a process known as leaching. Afterwards, the water was drawn off and boiled, which required more wood and coal, as well as being treated with such odious substances as human urine, brought from as far away as London. As crystals of precious alum began to form, the process was completed with a purification stage before the end product was packed for dispatch.

Alum had many uses but was chiefly in demand as a fixative for dyes, as it promoted deep colours on cloth, which became colour-fast after washing. The Italians had a virtual monopoly on the trade until the alum shale of Yorkshire was exploited from 1600. However, the local industry went into a sudden decline when other sources of alum, and more advanced dyestuffs, were discovered from 1850. The long and involved process of quarrying, burning, leaching, boiling, crystallising and purifying

The Rosedale Ironstone Railway seen at the top of Rosedale Chimney Bank (Walk 30)

was replaced by simpler, cheaper and faster production methods. Two dozen sites are scattered across the landscape where the industry once flourished. Look upon these stark remains, consider the toil and labour and bear in mind that it all took place so that fine ladies and gentlemen could wear brightly coloured clothes!

Jet

Jet, often known as Whitby jet, has been used to create ornaments and jewellery since the Bronze Age. It is found around the North York Moors, often along the coast, but also far inland around Carlton Bank. Jet is a type of coal, but it is peculiar because it formed from isolated logs of driftwood rather than from the thick masses of decayed vegetation that form regular coal seams. High-quality jet is tough and black, can be turned on a lathe or carved and takes a high polish. Jet has been used to create everything from intricately carved statuettes to shiny beads and facetted stones for jewellery. Jet crafting has long centred on Whitby, with peak production years being in the 19th century.

Ironstone

Cleveland ironstone was mined and quarried from around 500BC, as evidenced by an ancient bloomery site (where malleable iron is produced directly from iron ore) on Levisham Moor. Large-scale working didn't commence until around 1850, when coastal and moorland locations, such as Skinningrove and Rosedale, were exploited. As the steelworks developed, the tiny coastal village

NORTH YORK MOORS INDUSTRIES

of Skinningrove became known as the Iron Valley. Ironstone from Rosedale was transported over the moors by rail to the blast furnaces in Middlesbrough. Huge quantities of coal had to be shipped to the area, as industry and commerce were hungry for the iron that was produced. The last local ironstone mine, at North Skelton, closed in 1964. The number of steelworks in Middlesbrough has greatly reduced, while Skinningrove only just manages to remain in production.

Fishing and whaling

The coastal towns and villages thrived on fishing, especially herring fishing, until stocks dwindled. In Whitby, mainly from the mid-18th to mid-19th centuries, the fishing fleets turned their attention to whaling. Whalers often spent months at sea and didn't always return with a catch, but when they did, regular catches would bring great wealth to the town. Whale blubber was rendered for its oil, which was highly prized because when it burned it gave a bright and fairly soot-free light. Whenever the fishing settlements fell on hard times, smuggling provided an alternative form of employment, most notably at Robin Hood's Bay.

Grouse shooting

Some visitors imagine that the moors have always been there and represent the true wilderness qualities of the area, but this is untrue.

The moors have been man-managed over a long period of time and will only continue to exist with year-round maintenance. The uniform heather moorlands are largely a 19th-century creation, managed entirely for the sport of grouse shooting.

The red grouse, essentially a British bird, is tied to the heather moorlands on which it depends for food and shelter. Walkers know it for its heart-stopping habit of breaking cover from beneath their feet, then flying low while calling, 'go back, go back, go back'. It is a wonderfully camouflaged bird, spending all its time in the heather. Grouse graze on young heather shoots but need deep heather for shelter. Natural moorlands present a mosaic of vegetation types, but as the sport of grouse shooting developed in the 19th century, it became clear that a uniform heather habitat, which favours the grouse above all other species, would result in much greater numbers of birds to shoot.

Moorland management required vegetation to be burnt periodically, and as heather seeds are more fire-resistant than other seeds, heather cover quickly became dominant. Drainage ditches were also dug to dry out boggy ground and encourage further heather growth. Heather was burnt and regrown in rotation to provide short heather for feeding and deep 'leggy' heather for shelter. Gamekeepers were employed to shoot or trap 'vermin', so that grouse could flourish free of predators; however, it remains difficult to control intestinal parasites that often result in the birds being in poor condition. Harsh winters and cold wet springs can also cause devastating losses among the grouse population. What's more, old paths used by shooting parties have been widened for vehicular use, sometimes rather insensitively.

Come the Glorious Twelfth, or 12 August, the grouse-shooting season opens with teams of beaters driving the grouse towards the shooters, who station themselves behind shooting butts. Some moorlands charge very high prices for a day's shooting, and shoots are very much a social occasion. Walkers who despise blood sports should, nevertheless, bear in mind that without grouse shooting the moors would not be managed and would revert to scrub. A lot of moorland has been lost to forestry and agriculture, and managing the moors for shooting prevents further loss. What remains today is England's greatest unbroken expanse of heather moorland, and most visitors are keen to see it preserved.

North York Moors today

The North York Moors National Park Authority maintains an up-to-date website full of current contact information, events information and a comprehensive wealth of notes that go well beyond the scope of this guidebook. Be sure to check it in advance of any visit at www. northyorkmoors.org.uk

Boulder-studded heather on the lower slopes of Easterside Hill (Walk 10)

Moorsbus services link the towns with dales and remote moors

GETTING TO THE NORTH YORK MOORS

By air and sea
The nearest practical airports to the North York Moors are Leeds/Bradford and Teeside, although good rail connections allow ready access from the London airports and Manchester Airport. The nearest practical ferry ports are Hull and Newcastle.

By rail
Good rail connections from around the country serve the busy tourist resort of Scarborough throughout the day. To a lesser extent, Whitby can be reached by direct rail services from Middlesbrough, which would suit most travellers from the north-east. Other railway stations to consider include Malton, on account of its summer weekend Moorsbus services, and Saltburn, which connects with regular Arriva bus services. Check the National Rail website to plan journeys to and from the area, www.national rail.co.uk tel 03457 484950.

By bus
Daily National Express buses run to Scarborough and Whitby – www. nationalexpress.com. Daily Yorkshire Coastliner buses run from Leeds and York to Scarborough and Whitby – www.yorkbus.co.uk. Daily Arriva bus services from the north-east run to Guisborough, Whitby and Scarborough – www.arrivabus.co.uk/north-east. Daily East Yorkshire Motor Services buses run from Hull and the surrounding area to Scarborough – www.eyms.co.uk.

GETTING AROUND THE NORTH YORK MOORS

Moorsbus

The Moorsbus is a network of special low-cost bus services, often tying in with other bus and rail services to link some of the more popular little towns and villages with some of the more remote parts of the national park. Walkers who wish to make use of Moorsbus services should obtain a current timetable either from the national park authority or from tourist information centres. Timetables and places served tend to change each year, but as a general rule, services operate on summer Fridays, Saturdays, Sundays and Bank Holiday Mondays. It is essential to obtain up-to-date information, starting with the Moorsbus website, www.moorsbus.org

Buses

Other bus services are also available in the national park. Arriva buses run excellent regular daily services around the northern part of the North York Moors, as well as along the coast from Staithes to Whitby and Scarborough – www.arrivabus. co.uk/north-east. Scarborough & District buses cover the southern parts of the North York Moors, between Scarborough and Helmsley, and along the coast from Scarborough to Ravenscar, www.eyms.co.uk. Other operators include Transdev, which serves Helmsley from York, www. yorkbus.co.uk; Abbotts, which serves Osmotherley and Stokesley, www. abbottscoaches.co.uk; and Ryecat, which provides community transport to villages in the south of the national park, ryedalect.org.

The North Yorkshire Moors Railway provides nostalgic steam-hauled services

Rail

Following the closure of the coastal line in 1965, rail services have drastically reduced in the North York Moors. However, daily Northern trains run along the Eskdale line from Middlesbrough to Whitby, providing access to a series of fine walks in the northern part of the national park, www.northernrailway.co.uk. Seasonal steam-hauled services on the North Yorkshire Moors Railway, between Pickering and Goathland, catch the attention of walkers who want to enjoy a nostalgic railway journey to their walks, www.nymr.co.uk. All was not lost with the closure of the coastal railway, since the entire line between Scarborough and Whitby is now part of the National Cycle Route 1.

ACCOMMODATION

Accommodation options around the North York Moors National Park are abundant, but bear in mind that during the peak summer season it can still be difficult to secure lodgings, and in the depths of winter some places are not open. At the budget end there are plenty of campsites, although youth hostels are rather thin on the ground. Following closures in recent years there is now only Whitby, Boggle Hole, Scarborough, Lockton, Helmsley and Osmotherley.

Walkers looking for B&B, guest house or hotel accommodation will find plenty of choice in some areas, especially the coastal resorts, but little or nothing in some of the less-frequented dales further inland. However, every standard is available, from homely B&Bs and basic farmhouse accommodation, to luxury hotels with every facility and full meals services. On the whole, serviced accommodation in the North York Moors tends to be a little pricey, but with careful research reasonably priced options can be found, especially with Airbnb, www.airbnb.co.uk. The tourist information centres at Scarborough and Whitby may be aware of last-minute vacancies during busy periods.

FOOD AND DRINK

Most of the walking routes in this guidebook start and finish at places where food and drink is available. The starting point may be a town with plenty of pubs, restaurants and cafés, or it may be a village with a pub and a tearoom. There may be places en route that offer food and drink, such as wayside pubs and cafés, or there may be nothing at all. A note about the availability of refreshments is given in the information box at the beginning of each walk, although there is no guarantee that the places will be open when you need them! When booking accommodation be sure to enquire about meals, or to let your hosts know if you have any special dietary requirements. It goes without saying that you should be

The heathery expanse of Spaunton Moor from above Lastingham (Walk 29)

self-sufficient for food and drink for the duration of your walks.

WHEN TO WALK

Most visitors – and indeed too many visitors – explore the North York Moors during the summer months, and when the moors are flushed purple with heather and the air is sweetened with its scent, this can be a delightful time. But be warned that when the sun beats down on the moors there may be little shade, and the longer a heatwave lasts, the more the air tends to turn hazy, so that colour and depth are lost from the views. The spring and autumn months offer good walking conditions, with plenty of cool, clear days – often cool enough to ensure that you keep striding briskly! There is also less pressure

on accommodation and easier access to attractions along the way. In the winter months accommodation and transport are much reduced, and foul weather can sweep across the moors, which offer little shelter from wind or rain. However, there can be some exceptionally bright, clear days, and a dusting of snow on the landscape transforms the scene into something quite magical.

MAPS OF THE ROUTES

Extracts from the Ordnance Survey Landranger series of maps, at a scale of 1:50 000, are used throughout this guidebook, with overlays showing the routes. These extracts are adequate for navigation on the walks, but if you wish to explore more of the countryside off-route, and want to see exactly where you are in relation to other walking routes, then obtain the appropriate Ordnance Survey maps. The Landranger maps covering the North York Moors National Park include sheets 93, 94, 99, 100 and 101. Greater detail and clarity are available on Ordnance Survey Explorer maps, at a scale of 1:25 000. The relevant Explorer maps are OL26, covering the western half of the national park, and OL27, covering the eastern half of the national park. Bear in mind that these maps are printed on both sides, so that each sheet has a North and South side. The relevant Ordnance Survey maps for each walk are quoted in the information box introducing the walk. The starting points for the walks can be pinpointed using the six-figure Ordnance Survey grid references supplied. The BMC/Harvey map of the North York Moors covers all but six of the routes in this guidebook.

Access to the countryside
Use up-to-date maps, as dozens of rights of way have been officially diverted over the years, often to avoid farmyards or fields of crops. On the high moors walkers who are good map-readers will frequently notice that the clear path or track they are following is not actually a right of way, and that the right of way shown on the map is quite untrodden on the ground! For the most part, walkers are voting with their feet and have done so for many years, and landowners seem to accept the situation.

Large areas of open moorland have been designated as open access land under the Countryside and Rights of Way (CRoW) Act 2000. Open access land should not be regarded as offering unlimited access. Some areas are indeed open at all times, but others are restricted and can be closed for various reasons, including grouse shooting and the movement of animals. In some areas there may be a complete ban on dogs at any time, or it might be a requirement for dogs to be kept on a lead, particularly in areas where ground-nesting birds are present. It is a good idea to check whether any restrictions or closures are in force, which can be advised by the Open Access Contact Centre, tel 0300 0602091. Remember that access is granted on foot only and doesn't extend to bicycles or vehicles, nor does it imply any right to camp on a property. Also, remember that access to the area surrounding RAF Fylingdales is strictly forbidden.

NATIONAL PARK VISITOR CENTRES

There are two national park visitor centres in the North York Moors, and they perform the very important function of trying to interest visitors in and educate them about the necessary balance that needs to be struck between conservation and recreation in this fragile upland area. The busier of the two centres is beside the main road at the top of Sutton Bank, the

Ralph Cross is an ancient moorland marker and serves as the national park logo

quieter one is outside the little village of Danby in Eskdale. Both centres are full of information, dispensing maps, guidebooks and leaflets that cover walking opportunities, as well as presenting the history, heritage and natural history of the area. Audio-visual presentations are available, as well as guided walks with national park rangers. Both centres can be reached by Moorsbus services that operate at weekends during the summer.

- Sutton Bank National Park Centre, tel 01845 597426.
- The Moors National Park Centre, Danby, tel 01439 772737.

For administrative enquiries contact: North York Moors National Park Authority, The Old Vicarage, Bondgate, Helmsley, York, YO62 5BP, tel 01439 772700 www.northyork moors.org.uk.

TOURIST INFORMATION CENTRES

The main tourist information centres are on the coast at Scarborough and Whitby. These centres can help with various enquiries, including accommodation, attractions and transport.

- Town Hall, Nicholas Street, Scarborough, YO11 2HG, tel 01723 383636 www. discoveryorkshirecoast.com.
- Langbourne Road, Whitby, YO21 1DN, tel 01723 383636 www. discoveryorkshirecoast.com.

EMERGENCY SERVICES

No matter the nature of the emergency, if you require the police, ambulance, fire service, mountain rescue or coastguard, the number to dial is 999 (or European number 112). Be ready to give a full account of the nature of the emergency, and give your own phone number, so that they can stay in contact with you. Callers cannot request helicopter assistance, but based on the information supplied, someone will decide if one is needed. Always carry a basic first-aid kit to deal with minor incidents, be self-sufficient in terms of food and drink and dress in or pack the appropriate clothing to cope with all weather conditions. Those venturing on to exposed moorlands need the experience and skills to cope in such an environment, as well as the common sense to turn back if things get difficult or dangerous. Think about your actions and aim to walk safely.

USING THIS GUIDE

This guidebook contains details of 50 walking routes, spread all around the North York Moors National Park. Most are circular, so that anyone using a car can return to their vehicle at the end of the walk; however, a few are linear and require the use of public transport to complete them. Together, these routes cover almost 725km (450 miles) of rich and varied countryside, taking in some of the finest and most interesting features on and near the moors. The route summary table in Appendix A is provided to help you choose between the different routes.

Read the route descriptions carefully before setting out, and if carrying Ordnance Survey maps in addition to the extracts used in this book, be sure to take the ones listed for each walk. The essential information for each route is presented under standard headings.

Start/Finish: usually the same place, but sometimes different.

Distance/Ascent/Descent: given in kilometres, miles, metres and feet.

Time: duration of the walk, but not including time spent resting, eating, etc.

Terrain: summary of the nature of the terrain and the paths used.

Maps: OS Landranger and OS Explorer sheet numbers.

Refreshment: summary of pubs, restaurants and tearooms on the route.

Transport: summary of the available buses and/or trains serving the route.

GPX tracks

GPX tracks for the routes in this guidebook are available to download free at www.cicerone.co.uk/951/GPX. A GPS device is an excellent aid to navigation, but you should also carry a map and compass and know how to use them. GPX files are provided in good faith, but neither the author nor the publisher accepts responsibility for their accuracy.

The 'Surprise View' at Gillamoor stretches across Farndale to Spaunton Moor (Walk 7)

THE TABULAR HILLS

Forge Valley Woods is part of a National Nature Reserve (Walk 1)

THE TABULAR HILLS

The Tabular Hills stretch along the southern part of the North York Moors National Park. The land rises gently from south to north and is cut by a series of dales that leave tabular uplands between them. The gentle slopes often end abruptly at their northern ends in a series of shapely knolls, or nabs, that look out towards the rolling moorlands at the heart of the national park. From east to west, from Scarborough to Helmsley, the more prominent nabs include Barns Cliff, Langdale Rigg End, Blakey Topping, Whinny Nab, Levisham Moor, the Nab, Boonhill Common, Birk Nab, Helmsley Bank, Easterside Hill and Hawnby Hill. Prominent dales from east to west include the Forge Valley, Hole of Horcum, Newtondale, lower Rosedale, lower Farndale, Sleightholm Dale, Riccal Dale, Ash Dale, Beck Dale and lower Ryedale.

The rocks that make up the Tabular Hills are seldom exposed but belong to the Middle Oolite Group in the Corallian series of the Jurassic period and, hence, are around 170 million years old. They are essentially a limestone and lime-rich sandstone series, porous enough to allow surface water to drain away rapidly. In the more deeply cut dales the bedrock is formed from the older Oxford Clay, which is impervious and supports the flow of rivers and streams. Some areas of the Tabular Hills have been turned over to commercial forestry. The land is very fertile and easily ploughed but the soil is often too thin to support good root crops. However, grain crops such as wheat, barley and oats are grown in rotation, and oilseed rape blazes yellow early in summer.

As if to celebrate the distinct nature of these gentle heights, the waymarked Tabular Hills Walk has been established. It traverses the low hills and intervening dales from the coast at Scalby Mills to the bustling market town of Helmsley, a distance of 80km (50 miles). The signposts and waymarks for the route feature directional arrows and a Tabular Hills logo. The route has been designated a regional trail and is an initiative of the North York Moors National Park Authority.

Ten walking routes through the Tabular Hills are described, including two routes around Hackness, three in the Lockton and Levisham area and one each around Hutton-le-Hole, Gillamoor, Rievaulx Moor, Helmsley and Hawnby. Some of these take in the distinctive nabs, while others wander more through the dales. From time to time, on the higher ground, it is possible to look along the range and see how the higher nabs end abruptly, and the High Moors then stretch northwards into the heart of the North York Moors.

WALK 1

West Ayton, Hackness and the Forge Valley

Start/finish	Ye Olde Forge Valley Inn, West Ayton, SE 987 847
Distance	15km (9½ miles)
Total ascent/descent	240m (790ft)
Time	5hrs
Terrain	Easy walking along woodland paths and field paths, as well as farm tracks and minor roads
Maps	OS Landranger 101; OS Explorer OL27 South
Refreshments	Ye Olde Forge Valley Inn at West Ayton, East Ayton Lodge Hotel and Denison Arms at East Ayton, Everley Country House Café is off-route between Mowthorpe and Hackness, and Hackness Grange Hotel is off-route near Hackness
Transport	Regular Scarborough & District buses serve West and East Ayton from Scarborough, Pickering and Helmsley

The River Derwent once flowed straight from the moors to the sea, but at the end of the Ice Age its course was blocked and water overflowed, carving out the Forge Valley, which was later choked by wildwoods. These trees were harvested for charcoal to fuel small ironworks in the 14th century. The River Derwent repeatedly flooded the low-lying Vale of Pickering, so in the 18th century the Sea Cut was engineered to take the river along its original course to the sea. This walk explores the wooded Forge Valley, takes a look at the Sea Cut and offers the chance to visit the lovely estate village of Hackness.

Start at Ye Olde Forge Valley Inn at West Ayton. Follow the A170 road across the bridge to **East Ayton** and turn left along a road called Castlegate, signposted for the Forge Valley. Pass the East Ayton Lodge Hotel and walk down the road. Follow the road until a **public footpath** (not a public bridleway) is signposted on the right, flanked by fencing for a few paces. Walk up a broad woodland path parallel to a deep groove. Turn left near the top of the wooded slope and follow a path just inside **Ruston Cliff Wood**, with occasional views out across fields. Pass attractive pantiled stone buildings at **Osborne Lodge** and walk straight ahead. Fork left downhill, walking straight ahead to pass an information board.

FORGE VALLEY WOODS NATIONAL NATURE RESERVE

Towards the end of the Ice Age, around 10,000 years ago, a mass of stagnant ice dammed the broad valley, causing water to form the temporary Lake Hackness. This overflowed and carved the deep, steep-sided Forge Valley. The fields above the valley lie on soft Hambleton Oolite, while its sides are formed from hard Lower Calcareous Grit, and its floor is impervious Oxford Clay. The valley became choked with wildwoods, which in turn provided charcoal for small iron foundries in the 14th century. This is one of the best valley-side mixed deciduous woodlands in Yorkshire.

Continue along the path, eventually reaching a parking space at Green Gate. Turn left, then right down a road signposted for Hackness, where there is access to a viewpoint on the left at Hazel Head. Walk down the road to cross Mowthorpe Bridge over the Sea Cut.

THE SEA CUT

The River Derwent has its source on Fylingdales Moor, a mere spit and a throw from the North Sea. It begins by flowing towards the sea, but only 6km (4 miles) short of it, the river suddenly swings west and heads far inland. Its waters eventually spill into the North Sea via the Humber Estuary after a circuitous journey of 240km (150 miles). The Sea Cut, engineered by the distinguished inventor Sir George Cayley (a pioneer in the science of aerodynamics, amongst other things) in the early 18th century, diverts the headwaters of the River Derwent into Scalby Beck, passing floodwater straight into the sea instead of allowing it to inundate the Vale of Pickering.

Pass **Mowthorpe Farm** and walk a little way up the road, then turn right as indicated by a footpath sign. Go through a kissing gate and turn right to walk downhill

a little, then turn left to walk up a grassy groove along-side an old hedgerow. Go through a gate, then turn left up to another gate that gives access to **Hawthorn Wood**. Follow a clear path across and up the wooded slope, then walk beside a field to reach **Suffield Ings farm**, at around 160m (525ft). Keep to the right of the buildings as marked and leave along the farm access road. Keep straight on at a junction, but later, when the track swings right, leave it by following a path down to the left. This goes down a wooded valley and passes a crumbling limekiln. When a road is reached, turn left; it is hardly necessary to walk on the road, since as one path joins it, another heads off to the left. ▸

The path climbs a wooded slope, followed by a grassy slope, apparently for no other reason than to provide a fine view of **Hackness Hall**. Having achieved this aim, the path turns right downhill, crosses a stile and enters a wood, then runs gradually downhill across a slope. Leave the wood at another stile and contour across a grassy slope overlooking Mill Farm and the Derwent Valley. Turn right

The Sea Cut uses the original course of the River Derwent from Mowthorpe Bridge

Hackness village and Walk 2 are easily reached from here.

31

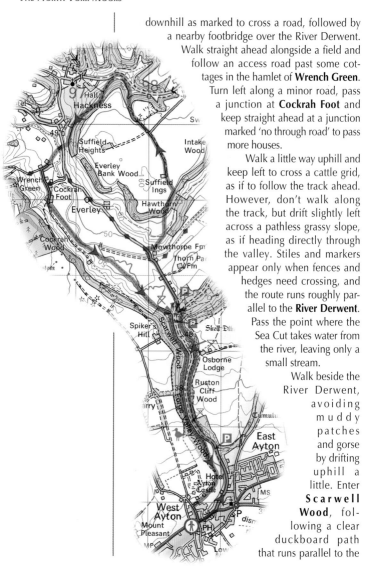

downhill as marked to cross a road, followed by a nearby footbridge over the River Derwent. Walk straight ahead alongside a field and follow an access road past some cottages in the hamlet of **Wrench Green**. Turn left along a minor road, pass a junction at **Cockrah Foot** and keep straight ahead at a junction marked 'no through road' to pass more houses.

Walk a little way uphill and keep left to cross a cattle grid, as if to follow the track ahead. However, don't walk along the track, but drift slightly left across a pathless grassy slope, as if heading directly through the valley. Stiles and markers appear only when fences and hedges need crossing, and the route runs roughly parallel to the **River Derwent**. Pass the point where the Sea Cut takes water from the river, leaving only a small stream.

Walk beside the River Derwent, avoiding muddy patches and gorse by drifting uphill a little. Enter **Scarwell Wood**, following a clear duckboard path that runs parallel to the river. You can gain access to a car park across a footbridge, where an information board illustrates local wildlife. If you do not require the car park, there is no need to cross the river, and the duckboard path can be followed further downstream through the **Forge Valley Woods**. The woodlands are dense and the undergrowth is lush, so the route is rather like a jungle trek!

The duckboard ends suddenly at a gate. Walk through a narrow meadow between the river and a wooded slope. Towards the end of the meadow, watch out for a track heading up to the right. Go through a gate and follow the grassy track past the tottering 14th-century ruins of **Ayton Castle**, then continue along a road past cottages at Castle Rise. Turn left down Yedmandale Road to return to the main road and Ye Olde Forge Valley Inn at **West Ayton**.

The duckboard riverside path through the jungle-like woods in the Forge Valley

WALK 2
Hackness, Broxa and Whisper Dales

Start/finish	Hackness Village Hall, SE 967 900
Distance	9.5km (6 miles)
Total ascent/descent	200m (655ft)
Time	3hrs
Terrain	Tracks and paths on wooded slopes and through fields
Maps	OS Landrangers 94 and 101; OS Explorer OL27 South
Refreshments	Hackness Grange Hotel is near the start
Transport	None

Hackness is a charming little village with a long history – the Abbess Hilda of Whitby chose a secluded site here to found a nunnery. A few quiet, charming and often unregarded little dales fan outwards from the village into surrounding forest, a couple of which are explored on this short walk. The route starts with a climb on to broad, cultivated Broxa Rigg, with a descent to Hard Dale and High Dales. After crossing Springwood Heights, the route continues through Whisper Dales, a sinuous grassy valley leading down to Low Dales on the return journey to Hackness.

Starting at Hackness Village Hall, walk up the road as if heading for the rest of the village, then double back sharp left up a track on a wooded slope. Keep right at a track junction to reach a grassy crest. Continue alongside **Chapman Banks Wood** for a while, then drift right to the other side of the vegetated crest, to locate a small gate hidden in a far corner. Go through the gate and keep to the edge of a field beside another wood, at around 160m (525ft). Look ahead to spot step-stiles from field to field and always keep to the edge, beside the wood. In the last field, aim for a farmhouse and go through a gate to reach a road.

Keep right of the buildings at **Broxa** to follow the farm road. Turn right and continue along a narrow, tarmac,

muck-and-manure road, passing a public footpath sign and heading in the direction of Broxa Forest. However, before reaching the forest, turn right as directed by another public footpath sign and walk across a field. Cross a step-stile among nettles into **Fewler Gate Wood** and follow a path down through a little wooded valley. Head right at the bottom, but watch for a stile on the left and step out into a field in Hard Dale. Go down to a stream and cross it, as indicated by a public footpath signpost. Walk uphill and turn left along a farm road.

The grassy track running downhill from Whisper Dales towards Low Dales

Just as a house is reached at **Newgate**, turn right uphill as indicated by a public footpath sign. Climb a grass-and-gorse bank, then enter a forest and turn left behind the house. Turn right steeply uphill and cross an old forest track to climb further. Leave the forest and walk alongside a field, continuing beside another stand of forest, at around 160m (525ft). Veer right along a very vague field path to go down into

35

another wood. Watch carefully for markers as some parts of the path are overgrown, especially when it is necessary to keep to the left-hand side of a fence. Step out into a field and head diagonally down it to reach a grassy track in **Whisper Dales** beside a stream flanked by trees.

Turn right to follow the grassy track down into **Low Dales**. It remains grassy and is marked by arrows for a while. Cross two footbridges beside two fords close together at **Lowdales Farm**. Follow a field path to the left of the road, as the road actually carries the full flow of water from **Lowdales Beck**! Continue to follow the path down through the dale to reach a junction. Left leads to St Peter's Church in **Hackness**, while right leads back to the road junction at the village hall, not far from the Hackness Grange Hotel.

HACKNESS

St Hilda founded a nunnery at Hackness in AD680, but even in this secluded setting it was discovered and plundered by the Danes in AD867, then rebuilt in the 11th century. An inscribed cross from the nunnery is located in St Peter's Church, but the only other reminder of those times is the village pond. Hackness is very much an estate village, and its main street is peculiar, as it has a vigorous stream running alongside it. Hackness Hall is a fine Georgian manor designed by John Carr, an architect from York. The hall is in the possession of Lord Derwent.

Hackness Hall and Hackness village lie just off-route

WALK 3

Lockton, Stain Dale, Saltergate and Levisham Moor

Start/finish	Lockton Youth Hostel, SE 845 900
Distance	20km (12½ miles)
Total ascent/descent	390m (1280ft)
Time	6hrs
Terrain	Generally easy, but a long walk; woodland tracks and field paths in the lower dales give way to higher moorland paths and tracks
Maps	OS Landranger 94; OS Explorer OL27 South
Refreshments	Horseshoe Inn at Levisham, Lockton Tea Rooms at Lockton, possible café at Saltersgate
Transport	Regular Yorkshire Coastliner buses serve Lockton and Saltergate from Pickering and Whitby.

Lockton and Levisham lie within easy reach of deep dales and open moorlands. This fine, long walk leaves Lockton and drops down into Stain Dale, then later climbs to reach strangely sculpted rocks at the Bridestones. Newgate Brow and Saltergate Brow allow wide-ranging views across the moors and dales. An easy walk over Levisham Moor leads to the charming stone village of Levisham, which surrounds a spacious green. The last stretch of the the walk crosses a deep, wooded dale on the return to Lockton.

Leave Lockton and its little youth hostel by heading for the **A169** road, as if going directly to Saltergate. ▶ Cross the main road to enter a field. Don't follow the grassy track alongside it, but strike diagonally right across the field. If there is no trodden path, keep to the right of a **pylon** to find a track leading down through a gate. Go down the track into a wood and pass through a couple more gates. Watch carefully, as the route avoids Staindale Lodge in the following manner: turn right as marked up a grassy slope, turn right up an access road to a gate and stile, turn left to follow a track through a wood, then just

If arriving by bus, the bus stop is beside the main road.

before reaching a cattle grid, turn left to cross a stile and walk down to **Staindale Lodge**. Keep to the right of out-buildings, cross a ladder stile and turn right along a track.

Follow a grassy path through **Holm Woods**, then continue walking through meadows in **Stain Dale**. Use power line poles as guides when looking ahead to spot gates and stiles. Pass to the right of buildings at **Low Staindale**, then climb a little to find a grassy track and follow it down to ford a stream. Turn left to go through a kissing gate and enter little Dovedale, with its ancient oak woodland and flower-rich grasslands. Cross a little footbridge over **Dovedale Griff** and walk along the grassy floor of the dale. Cross another little footbridge and follow a stone-paved path up a ridge called Needle Point, which is sparsely wooded, with a lush ground cover of heather and bilberry. The path levels out and runs through a groove in the heather, then a sandy path leads to the **Bridestones**, at around 200m (655ft). Turn

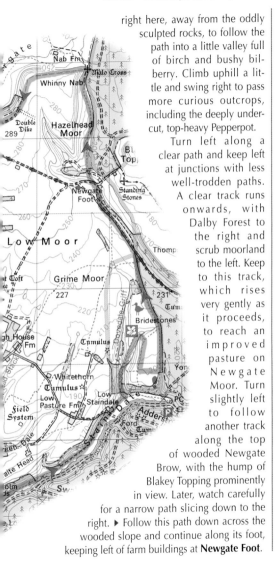

right here, away from the oddly sculpted rocks, to follow the path into a little valley full of birch and bushy bilberry. Climb uphill a little and swing right to pass more curious outcrops, including the deeply undercut, top-heavy Pepperpot.

Turn left along a clear path and keep left at junctions with less well-trodden paths. A clear track runs onwards, with Dalby Forest to the right and scrub moorland to the left. Keep to this track, which rises very gently as it proceeds, to reach an improved pasture on Newgate Moor. Turn slightly left to follow another track along the top of wooded Newgate Brow, with the hump of Blakey Topping prominently in view. Later, watch carefully for a narrow path slicing down to the right. ▶ Follow this path down across the wooded slope and continue along its foot, keeping left of farm buildings at **Newgate Foot**.

An old stone gatepost partly buried in the undergrowth helps identify it.

39

The top-heavy Pepperpot is one of the natural Bridestones sculptures

Cross stiles on either side of the access road and turn left along a grassy terrace. Watch carefully for a small gate on the right and walk down through a squelchy field to a large gate. Follow a path that gradually drifts away from a forest, going through more gates as a couple of big fields give way to bracken moorland. Continue until you reach the prominent leaning stone pillar of **Malo Cross** at a junction of paths.

Turn left alongside a fence as the path rises gradually from a slope of scrub woodland and bracken to the top of a fine grassy brow. Alternatively, climb straight from the stone cross on to **Whinny Nab**, at 296m (971ft), then continue along the brow. Either way, keep walking along the grassy brow, with views down to the former Saltersgate Inn. Go through a gate beside a shelter belt of trees. Turn left to follow a path running parallel to a track, reaching a farm road. Turn right along this to reach the busy **A169** road. ◄

A national park information van might be parked nearby in summer.

Cross the road with care and turn right along a path to reach a gap at the head of the **Hole of Horcum**, above a sharp bend on the main road. Go through a gate and follow a moorland track a short way uphill that soon levels out at around 270m (885ft) on **Levisham Moor**. There is only one clear track across the undulating

THE LEGENDARY SALTERSGATE INN

Saltergate was an important trading route running inland from the coast. It was also known as the 'Salt Road' or 'Fish Road'. Smugglers carrying illicit goods along the road would often hole up at the Saltersgate Inn. According to local lore, revenue men raided the inn one night, but the smugglers ensured that nothing was discovered. However, one revenue man who lingered too long afterwards was killed and his body buried beneath the hearthstone of the inn. The landlord of the day insisted that a fire was kept alight to deter anyone from digging up the hearthstone, and this tradition was maintained for generations afterwards. The ever-blazing fire at the inn became a tourist attraction in its own right! Alas, the fire burns no longer and the inn closed in 2007. There is a plan to demolish the inn and build a café and small brewery.

heather moorland, so route-finding errors are unlikely, even though the area is quite featureless. Small cast-iron plaques mark features of interest along the way. Tiny **Seavy Pond** and **Dundale Pond**, which were dug in medieval times as watering-holes for livestock, can be easily passed by unseen, as they are choked with vegetation.

The track crosses a gap at the latter, where there is a five-fingered signpost. Walk a short way uphill to leave

The leaning stone pillar of Malo Cross and the rounded hump of Whinny Nab

the moorland at a gate, where it becomes a tarmac road, Limpsey Gate Lane, leading down into the attractive and spacious village of **Levisham**. Keep walking down the road to the bottom end of the village. Follow a path straight downhill, cutting out a sweeping bend to land on the road at a lower level. Turn left down the road to pass **Levisham Mill Farm**, deep in the valley. Climb up the steep road to return to **Lockton**.

LEVISHAM AND LOCKTON

Levisham boasts a broad central green surrounded by stout stone cottages and farmhouses. Facilities include the Horseshoe Inn for food, drink and accommodation, as well as Rectory Farm B&B. There is a youth hostel at nearby Lockton across the valley, as well as the Lockton Tea Rooms. The road between the two villages features 1:5 gradients on both sides of the valley.

Houses in Levisham face onto a broad, open green.

WALK 4

Levisham and the Hole of Horcum

Start/finish	Horseshoe Inn, Levisham, SE 833 906
Distance	10km (6¼ miles)
Total ascent/descent	260m (855ft)
Time	4hrs
Terrain	Valley-side paths cross steep wooded slopes as well as gentler moorland slopes, with easier field paths towards the end; generally easy
Maps	OS Landranger 94 or 100; OS Explorer OL27 South
Refreshments	Horseshoe Inn at Levisham, possible café at Saltersgate
Transport	None, but regular Yorkshire Coastliner buses serve Lockton and Saltergate from Pickering and Whitby, and Levisham Railway Station offers an alternative starting point from the North Yorkshire Moors Railway.

The village of Levisham is reached only after negotiating 1:5 (20%) gradient roads, and anyone going there by car has to leave the same way. Deep, steep-sided valleys flank Levisham Moor, while the Hole of Horcum is a remarkable dalehead that was carved by glacial melt-water at the end of the Ice Age. Most visitors come and go using the main road over Saltergate Bank, but the Hole of Horcum can be reached by using valley-side paths from Levisham. The return to Levisham overlooks part of the North Yorkshire Moors Railway.

Leave the Horseshoe Inn at the top end of Levisham and walk straight down through the village, admiring the stone houses that surround the broad central green. Walk to the bottom end of the village and follow a path straight downhill. Turn left along a footpath that swings across a wooded slope. Later, climb 60 steps, then fork left at a junction along a path signposted for Horcum. The path is quite narrow and flanked by flowers, brambles and bracken, with views across the valley to the nearby village of Lockton.

The path swings left as it works its way through the valley, and it is well wooded at times along Levisham Brow. Generally, the path runs gradually downhill and the woods begin to thin out. Go through a small gate and cut across a slope of bracken to reach the side-valley of Dundas Griff. A signpost points ahead to Saltergate and a small stream has to be forded before you cross **Levisham Beck** using a footbridge.

Follow the path gently uphill, across the wooded valley side, using a boardwalk before going through a gate. Continue along a path across the grassy valley

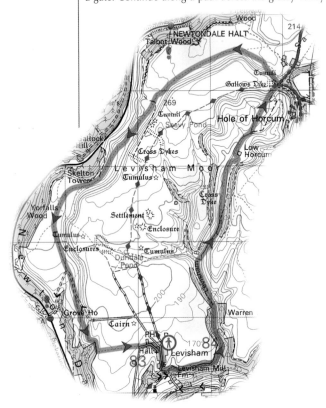

A clear path climbs up through the heathery head of the Hole of Horcum

Grazing on the moorland shelf near Skelton Tower

side, and later keep to the left of a building at **Low Horcum**. Walk onwards and head down a grassy track to go through a gate. A clear path leads up through heather, then rises more steeply up a heathery groove as it climbs out of the **Hole of Horcum**. Enjoy the views around this splendid hollow before continuing through a gate at the top to see a bend in the busy **A169** road on Saltergate Bank. ◄

There might be a new café below.

According to a locally favoured legend, a giant by the name of Wade was out of sorts with his wife, and so he scooped up a pile of earth to throw at her. He missed, and the resulting hole became the **Hole of Horcum**, while the lump of earth became Blakey Topping. The former Saltersgate Inn can be seen from the gap at the head of the Hole of Horcum. The strange pyramidal radar at RAF Fylingdales rises beyond, looking quite out of place in the bleak moorland setting.

See Walk 3 for a quick return to Levisham.

A gate gives access to a track rising from the gap. ◄ Go through the gate, but turn immediately right to cross a stile and slant left downhill. Walk across a grassy moor, but don't stray too far from the steep slopes of **Levisham Moor**. Follow a vague path, which becomes much clearer later, but take the time to identify the path instead of forging straight through the heather. Further ahead there is more bracken, and there are views down on to the North Yorkshire Moors Railway in the deep gorge of Newtondale. A short detour can be made to the little ruin of **Skelton Tower**, which is a good viewpoint overlooking the gorge, but make sure to return to the main path afterwards to avoid wet ground beyond. The broad, grassy path eventually reaches a bend on a minor road above **Levisham Railway Station**. ▶

Walk up the road, but only to pass a small wood. Branch off to the right, but fork left almost immediately to follow a grassy path. Further along, turn left up another clear grassy path, climbing a slope covered in gorse bushes. Turn around the top of a small, steep-sided wooded valley, then walk alongside a couple of large fields. Follow a narrow road straight into **Levisham** to return to the Horseshoe Inn.

The station offers an alternative starting point.

Skelton Tower overlooks Newtondale and the North Yorkshire Moors Railway

47

WALK 5

*Levisham Station, Levisham and
Newton-on-Rawcliffe*

Start/finish	Levisham Railway Station, SE 818 910
Distance	9.5km (6 miles)
Total ascent/descent	260m (855ft)
Time	3hrs
Terrain	Generally easy, using clear roads and tracks for most of the way, with a steep, vague and muddy path at the end
Maps	OS Landranger 94 or 100; OS Explorer OL27 South
Refreshments	Horseshoe Inn at Levisham, Mucky Duck at Newton-on-Rawcliffe.
Transport	The North Yorkshire Moors Railway serves Levisham Railway Station; Monday-only Ryecat buses serve Newton-on-Rawcliffe from Pickering.

Levisham Railway Station is on the North Yorkshire Moors Railway – a line that operates nostalgic steam-hauled trains through the heathery heart of the North York Moors National Park. The station lies deep in the dale, well below the village of Levisham, and even less conveniently at the foot of a steep slope from the village of Newton-on-Rawcliffe. This short circular walk climbs from Levisham Station to Levisham, then runs down a wooded valley to Farwath. After climbing to Newton-on-Rawcliffe, the route drops steeply back to the station.

Leave Levisham Railway Station by following the road as if for Levisham village, but only to pass **Grove Lodge**. Just as the road begins to steepen, head off to the right through a small gate and follow a path up a wooded slope. Walk up a field to go through a gate at the top, then turn right. Almost immediately, fork left up a grassy path on a slope of gorse bushes. Turn around the top of a small, steep-sided wooded valley, then walk alongside a couple of big fields, at around 190m (625ft). Follow a narrow road into

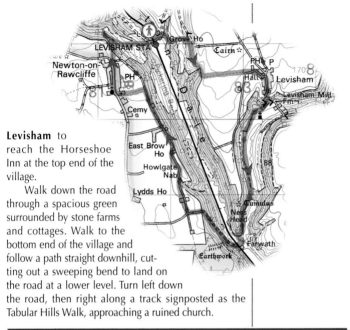

Levisham to reach the Horseshoe Inn at the top end of the village.

Walk down the road through a spacious green surrounded by stone farms and cottages. Walk to the bottom end of the village and follow a path straight downhill, cutting out a sweeping bend to land on the road at a lower level. Turn left down the road, then right along a track signposted as the Tabular Hills Walk, approaching a ruined church.

LEVISHAM CHURCH

St Mary's Church stands on an 11th-century foundation and is tucked deep in a steep-sided valley. It seems rather remote from Levisham village. According to legend it was supposed to be built in the village, but each night the devil carried all the building materials down into the valley! The church was virtually abandoned before the tower was added, and a new church was built in 1884 at a more convenient location in the village.

The route varies from a muddy woodland track to a grassy path, passing through a succession of gates and eventually reaching a three-way signpost in a field. Turn left and pass through two gates to cross two footbridges: the first one crosses a drain; the second crosses Levisham Beck. The marshy grassland near the beck is the Hagg Wood Marsh Nature Reserve, where

49

Houses in the village of Levisham face on to a sloping green

alkaline waters allow an interesting assemblage of plants to flourish. Turn right to walk through a farmyard at **Farwath**, crossing the North Yorkshire Moors Railway at a level crossing.

Cross another footbridge, or culvert bridge, over **Pickering Beck** and follow the clear farm access road of Farwath Road up across a wooded slope. It emerges at a junction of farm access roads where a right turn leads past Howlgate Farm and **Howlgate Nab**. Keep to the farm access road to pass **East Brow House**. Eventually a public footpath sign points left. Turn left and walk through a field and along a path leading to St John's Church. Turn right to follow a road through **Newton-on-Rawcliffe**, where the Mucky Duck pub faces a duck pond.

Follow the road to the top of the village and keep to a grassy track just to the right of a stone seat, as sign-posted for Cropton. Cross a rise at 190m (625ft) and drop down past a building, descending a steep hollow-way on a wooded slope. Watch for a stile on the right, cross it and head off to the right, descending very gradually across the slope into **Newtondale**, looking out for a gate. Go through the gate and veer left, looking into the valley to spot **Levisham Railway Station**, then take the path that leads off the grassy slope and steeply down a wooded slope, which can be muddy when wet. Cross a footbridge to return to the station.

NORTH YORKSHIRE MOORS RAILWAY

This scenic railway runs between Pickering and Grosmont, a distance of 29km (18 miles), and is famous for its steam-hauled services, although when it first opened in 1836 the carriages were pulled by horses between Pickering and Whitby. George Stephenson engineered the line, but it had to be improved considerably by George Hudson before steam trains could use it. The line was closed in 1964, then reopened by dedicated railway enthusiasts, and is now an immensely popular tourist attraction. Scenes from the line have featured regularly in films and television, including the *Heartbeat* TV series and *Harry Potter* films.

The Mucky Duck pub and the little village duckpond at Newton-on-Rawcliffe

WALK 6

Hutton-le-Hole, Lastingham, Cropton and Appleton-le-Moors

Start/finish	Ryedale Folk Museum, Hutton-le-Hole, SE 705 900
Distance	15km (9½ miles)
Total ascent/descent	260m (855ft)
Time	5hrs
Terrain	Easy walking along low-level paths, tracks and roads, brushing moorland slopes first, then returning through fields later
Maps	OS Landranger 94 or 100; OS Explorers OL26 and 27 South
Refreshments	Pub and tearooms at Hutton-le-Hole, pubs at Lastingham, Cropton and Appleton-le-Moors
Transport	Summer weekend Moorsbus services to Hutton-le-Hole from Pickering and Danby; Monday, Wednesday and Saturday Ryecat buses serve Hutton-le-Hole, Lastingham, Cropton and Appleton-le-Moors from Pickering

The three little villages of Hutton-le-Hole, Lastingham and Cropton sit where the Tabular Hills give way to the High Moors. True to form the Tabular Hills display a series of high nabs before the higher moors stretch their uniform heather slopes northwards. This walk links all three villages, then uses the course of the waymarked Tabular Hills Walk to take in a fourth village, Appleton-le-Moors, on the way back to Hutton-le-Hole. Each village has at least a pub offering food and drink, so this is an ideal walk for those who like to be pampered.

Leave the Ryedale Folk Museum in Hutton-le-Hole and walk down the road a short way to the village hall. Across the road from the hall is a public footpath sign beside a small gate. Follow this path across fields as marked, then cross a footbridge over Loskey Beck and follow a woodland path up through a gate, continuing along a grassy

The Millennium Stone above the village of Lastingham

track to reach a road. Turn right along the road – but well before reaching a road junction, watch for a public footpath sign pointing left along a grassy track. Follow the track through a gate, noting that some stretches are wet and muddy, then swing right and continue alongside a fence. Cut across a grassy slope as marked, well above **Camomile Farm**. Drop down into a valley where the ground is wet enough to support bog myrtle. Climb up the other side to reach a clear track above the village of **Lastingham**, beside its Millennium Stone and a signpost.

> The little village of **Lastingham** is huddled between the Tabular Hills and High Moors and can easily be explored by making a detour from the route. Of particular interest is St Mary's Church, with its Norman crypt and Shrine of St Cedd, originally built in 1078 on the site of an ancient Celtic monastery. Food and drink are available from the Lastingham Grange Hotel and Blacksmith's Arms.

Walk past the Millennium Stone and follow a track signposted for Hartoft. This quickly becomes a broad, grassy track running alongside a drystone wall. The track rises gently, then runs downhill, with moorland to the left and fields to the right, eventually fording Tranmire

Beck. Head straight uphill to a corner of a wall and follow the wall onwards, using a narrow grassy path to reach a clear farm access road near **High Askew**. Turn right to walk down the road, which eventually reaches a road junction.

Turn left, as signposted, along a public footpath, pass through a gate in a hedge and continue down a field before turning right alongside the River Seven. Go through a gate on to a road and turn left across a bridge. Follow the road away from the river, up past **Beckhouse Farm**, then down to a junction. Turn right over another bridge and walk up the road towards **Cropton**. Either walk all the way up the road to reach the village and its pub, or omit the village and turn right along a clear track signposted as the Tabular Hills Walk.

The Tabular Hills Walk follows a clear track, but when this track suddenly turns right, leave it by walking straight ahead to enjoy a fine, garlic-scented woodland path, passing through a number of gateways. Eventually, at a junction of paths turn right down to the River Seven

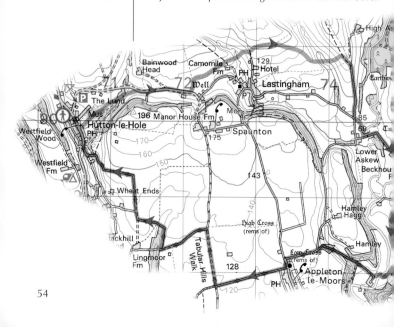

CROPTON

A motte and bailey was built at Cropton in the 12th century, but it was in ruins by the end of the 14th century. St Gregory's Church may have been built on a Norman chapel site, but while it retains its 12th-century font, the building is essentially a 19th-century restoration. The New Inn offers accommodation, food and drink and a campsite, as well as tours of its microbrewery. Other lodgings are available around the village.

and cross it using a footbridge. Rise to a small gate, then follow a farm access road uphill, away from Appleton Mill Farm and continue along Hamley Lane. Turn left at a road junction beside the stump of an old stone cross to approach **Appleton-le-Moors**. The route turns right just as it reaches the substantial Dweldapilton Hall on the outskirts of the village.

APPLETON-LE-MOORS

Appleton-le-Moors is a typical Yorkshire 'croft and toft' village. The crofts are the little cottages arranged on either side of the long main street; the tofts are the pieces of land extending from the back of each dwelling, where householders would grow their own vegetables. The imposing Dweldapilton Hall was built by a wealthy whaler, Dweldapilton being an earlier name for the village. The Moors Inn offers food, drink and accommodation.

Follow the track away from the hall, eventually reaching a prominent junction of tracks. Walk through a gate and approach a wood where you will see two gates ahead – be sure to go through the gate on the right into the wood. Turn right to walk around the inside edge of the wood, then continue through fields. Turn right along another clear track, Bottomfields Lane, which rises gently. Turn left at the top and continue along a grassy track through more fields. The track then becomes narrow and drops steeply, passing through a gate and down to a road. Turn right to walk back up into the charming village of **Hutton-le-Hole**.

Hutton-le-Hole has a long history of settlement dating back to Neolithic times. The village was mentioned in the Domesday Book as 'Hoton', but throughout the ages it has also been known as as 'Hege-Hoton', 'Hoton under Heg' and 'Hewton'. As a placename Hutton-le-Hole dates only from the 19th century. The village features the Ryedale Folk Museum, Crown Inn, tearooms, accommodation and gift shops.

RYEDALE FOLK MUSEUM

Trace the history of Yorkshire folk from 4000BC to 1953, with plenty of hands-on exhibits, as you wander from one part of the museum site to another. Over a dozen buildings have been erected since 1964, some with roofs supported by enormous cruck frames (pairs of curved wooden timbers supporting the ends of the roof), some standing in isolation, while others are arranged as a row of small shops. Vintage vehicles, including motorised and horse-drawn carriages, are preserved, and land around the site sprouts vegetables and flowers, including many varieties of cornfield flowers. Local folk often give demonstrations of traditional crafts while wearing period dress. There is an entrance charge, and the museum incorporates a shop and toilets, tel 01751 417367 www.ryedalefolkmuseum.co.uk.

Sheep regularly graze the extensive green in the middle of Hutton-le-Hole

WALK 7

Gillamoor, Boonhill Common and Fadmoor

Start/finish	Royal Oak, Gillamoor, SE 682 899
Distance	8km (5 miles)
Total ascent/descent	140m (460ft)
Time	2hrs 30mins
Terrain	Easy walking along woodland and field paths with linking roads.
Maps	OS Landranger 94 or 100; OS Explorer OL26 South
Refreshments	Royal Oak at Gillamoor
Transport	Monday-only Ryecat buses serve Gillamoor and Fadmoor from Pickering

Gillamoor and Fadmoor are quiet, charming little villages with neat, spacious greens, several stone farms and cottages. Both villages are surrounded by fields that rise gradually to Boonhill Common, which is another of the nabs on the Tabular Hills, beyond which stretch extensive heather moorlands. Despite being flanked by the River Dove and Hodge Beck, Gillamoor and Fadmoor, in most respects, lacked a constant supply of water. This problem was overcome when lengthy leats were constructed to channel water to both villages from distant sources.

Start from the Royal Oak in Gillamoor and walk through the village to reach St Aidan's Church. The road runs left of the church and reaches the Surprise View that overlooks the River Dove and Spaunton Moor. As the road bends left, immediately branch left along a signposted footpath that runs along the inside edge of a woodland at the top of a steep brow. The path continues alongside a field, then heads straight for a minor road. Turn right to follow the road past a junction, as signposted for Bransdale, beside **Dial Farm**. Walk down a wooded road that levels out among fields and passes **Grays Farm**. Turn left along a narrow road marked 'no through road' and

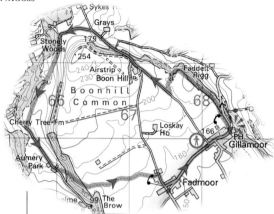

follow it around the lower slopes of **Boonhill Common**, heading downhill a short way.

Head left from the road to follow a signposted bridleway that starts out as a grassy track running down past a gate. Walk up through another gate to enter fields and look back to admire the fine house at **Stonely Woods**.

A little cottage standing beside the broad central green in the village of Fadmoor

Walk alongside fields and fences, passing through gates as marked, to land on another narrow road above **Cherry Tree Farm**. Turn left to cross a cattle grid and walk past a farm at **Aumery Park**. Just as you leave the last building, turn left up through a gate and walk alongside a fence as signposted for Fadmoor. The fence leads up across a wooded slope, and the path continues across a higher wooded slope with tangled brambly ground cover. Watch out for a gate on the left, at the top of **The Brow**, leading out into fields.

The pleasant valley of the River Dove below Gillamoor

Walk diagonally across the fields, and if no trodden path can be discerned, look ahead to spot the required step-stiles and take note of the direction given by marker arrows at each one. When you reach a road at some farm buildings, turn right to walk into the village of **Fadmoor**, then turn left to cross the central green to leave the village. The road continues straight ahead to return to **Gillamoor**.

GILLAMOOR AND FADMOOR

These two charming little villages lacked a reliable water supply until the 18th century. Joseph Foord engineered a lengthy aqueduct, or leat, tapping into distant sources of water to channel a supply to the villages. This supply was still used even into the 20th century, until it was replaced by piped water. The Royal Oak offers food, drink and accommodation in Gillamoor.

WALK 8

Newgate Bank, Rievaulx Moor and Helmsley Bank

Start/finish	Newgate Bank car park, SE 564 890
Distance	17km (10½ miles)
Total ascent/descent	230m (755ft)
Time	5hrs 30mins
Terrain	Good forest and moorland tracks give way to farm tracks and field paths; some vague forest paths require careful route-finding
Maps	OS Landranger 100; OS Explorer OL26 South
Refreshments	None on the route, but plenty of choice at nearby Helmsley
Transport	Summer weekend Moorsbus services pass Newgate Bank between Helmsley and Bilsdale

The Tabular Hills rise so high and heathery on Rievaulx Moor and Helmsley Bank that they seem to challenge the wide moorland expanses further north. On a clear day extensive views can be enjoyed from the high brow of Helmsley Bank, although on this walk views are lost when the route descends into dense forest. After traversing high above wooded Riccal Dale, the walk crosses forested Ash Dale and Beck Dale. Careful route-finding is required along a rather vague and indistinct forest path before clear farm tracks and roads complete the circuit.

The Forestry Commission car park, off the B1257 at Newgate Bank, offers a small viewing platform, but there are better views to be enjoyed later. Just as the forest access road leaves the main road, a footpath signpost points straight along a clear forest track. Follow it, noting the bramble-tangled ground cover. Leave the forest and continue along the track with forest to the left and the heather expanse of **Rievaulx Moor** to the right.

The clear track rises gradually, offering fine views of Bilsdale and the extensive moors on either side of it, with

the Cleveland Hills clustered around the dalehead. Pass a trig point at 328m (1076ft) on Helmsley Bank, above Roppa Wood, and continue down the gently sloping track to cross a minor road. Benches are available at a viewpoint that offers an extensive vista northwards across the High Moors.

Looking across Bilsdale from high on Rievaulx Moor

Keep walking onwards, following another gentle downhill track along the brow. There are views for a short while before the track runs deep into a forest, where there is a mixture of tree species, and the walking is pleasant. Always keep to the clearest track, which heads gently downhill, and take in the views wherever there has been clear-felling. Later, you will see a couple of viewpoint benches off to the left, overlooking the High Moors, Birk Nab and Riccal Dale.

The track reaches a car park and a road. Walk across the road, and a little to the left, to find a barrier gate and an overgrown forest path leading onwards. While this isn't actually a right of way, it is in regular use by walkers and horse-riders. Follow the track, which provides glimpses of Riccal Dale down to the left. Avoid a right turn, but keep right soon afterwards to follow a muddy track gently down into denser forest. This track swings right from the forest as part of the Tabular Hills Walk and runs along the edge, where it is firm and grassy, with views across the fields surrounding **Carlton Park Farm**.

Cross a road to see a public footpath sign pointing along a gravel track for **Carlton Grange**. Walk straight past the house, then go through a gate and turn left as marked alongside a field. Turn right and cross a step-stile to leave the field, then veer right down a grassy track into Ash Dale. ◄ Note some fine straight pines in the dale. Climb up the other side and follow a track to **High Baxton's Farm**. Turn left along a road to walk a field's length, then turn right through a gate, signposted as a public footpath, to leave the road.

Do not follow a path accompanying a power line across the dale.

Walk alongside a field and turn right, then turn left across a step-stile and walk alongside another field. Go through a gate and walk to the corner of the next field. Pass through another gate and cross a forest track, to pick up and follow a path downhill. The path is clear and obvious and surfaced with soft pine needles. It leads down into jungle-like Beck Dale, where you will cross a streambed that is normally dry. Climb steeply uphill and follow a narrow path onwards, crossing over a forest track.

Take great care following the next stretch of the path, although there are occasional marker posts. Cross a grassy track and keep walking onwards, taking a meandering course to reach yet another grassy track. Turn right up this track, then left at a junction to follow a clearer track. This can be wet and muddy in places, but stick with it to reach a gate and leave the forest. Follow a grassy track alongside fields, crossing a dip to reach **Oscar Park Farm**. Go through the farmyard and follow the farm access road to the B1257. Turn right to follow the road, which has a wide grassy verge, and walk all the way back to **Newgate Bank**. Alternatively, flag down the summer weekend Moorsbus if it is due to pass.

Two trees seen in silhouette on Rievaulx Moor on the way up to Helmsley Bank

63

WALK 9
Helmsley, Beck Dale and Ash Dale

Start/finish	Market Place, Helmsley, SE 612 838
Distance	10.5km (6½ miles)
Total ascent/descent	150m (490ft)
Time	3hrs 15mins
Terrain	Easy woodland tracks and paths through the dales, linked by field paths over higher ground
Maps	OS Landranger 100; OS Explorer OL26 South
Refreshments	Plenty of pubs, restaurants and cafés around Helmsley
Transport	Helmsley is a Moorsbus hub with summer weekend services into the surrounding countryside; Scarborough & District buses run regularly to and from Pickering and Scarborough; Transdev buses link Helmsley with York

The steep-sided, forested dales of Beck Dale and Ash Dale, which are cut into the Tabular Hills, are on the very doorstep of the bustling market town of Helmsley, yet few visitors seem to be aware of them. Beck Dale is indeed drained by a little beck, while Ash Dale is generally dry. Both dales were essentially carved by torrents of glacial melt-water, and any water they carry today is a mere trickle compared with their past burden. Both dales are easily accessed from Helmsley and run parallel throughout their length. They are easily linked using field paths from one to the other.

Start at the Market Place in the middle of Helmsley and follow the Stokesley road out of town. This leads along Church Street, past All Saints Church, then along High Street, which further on has a beck running along its length. Keep on the right-hand side of the road, but avoid a turning marked as a private road. Turn right a little later, as signposted along a footpath, to follow a stone-paved path alongside a beck. Cross a little foot-bridge and continue upstream, soon following a clear track towards a sawmill site.

Keep following the track, which runs along the grassy floor of wooded Beck Dale. When a junction of tracks is reached, turn right as signposted along a footpath. Go through a pheasant enclosure and later follow the track as it crosses the beck. ▶ The track eventually runs out of room on the floor of the dale, climbs up the valley side and is signposted as a footpath. When a track junction is reached, turn left, not along the other track, but up a narrow path through conifers. This path soon runs level across a more open, forested brow with a ground cover of bracken and brambles.

Turn right along a track, then quickly right again through a little gate, followed by a left turn alongside a field. Go through a gate and walk alongside another field, cross a stile, then turn right and then left alongside the field to reach a road. Turn right along the road, away from **High Baxton's Farm**, for the space of one large field. Turn left off the road to follow a clear track down into wooded **Ash Dale**. Turn right to walk down along the floor of the valley, as signposted for Helmsley, with steep wooded slopes on either side. There is little way of gauging progress down the dale along a forest track, but when the steep bank on the right dwindles to nothing, watch for a narrow path slipping out of the woods through a gate on that side. Walk alongside a field and go through a gate. Turn right through fields to reach another gate, then turn left. Turn right round the field and left at another gate. The path joins a road at Warwick Place and continues into **Helmsley**. Turn right and left by road, then walk through the churchyard to finish back at Market Place.

Look out for squirrels and deer, as well as woodland birds. An abundance of pheasants are reared in Collier Hag Wood.

65

*Wheatfield near
High Baxton's Farm*

HELMSLEY

Helmsley is a quintessential Yorkshire market town that can trace its ancestry back to Anglo-Saxon times. The spacious Market Place fills with stalls on market day and serves as a car park at other times. As well as the Market Cross, there is a towering monument to the second Lord Feversham. Stout stone buildings stand on all sides of the Market Place, and a couple of poky alleys lined with quaint little shops lead away from the square. The most prominent building is the Town Hall. All Saints Church was founded in Norman times, but is essentially a 19th-century structure. Helmsley offers a good range of accommodation, banks with ATMs, a post office, toilets, plenty of pubs, restaurants and tea rooms, as well as shops galore, including an outdoor gear store.

DUNCOMBE PARK

Another fine attraction near Helmsley is Duncombe Park, home of Lord Feversham. Visitors are charged according to whether they just wish to explore the extensive Arcadian parkland, or include a visit to the garden and terraces, or embark on a guided tour of the large house at the centre of the park. There is also a tearoom and a thriving events calendar. Tel 01439 770213 www.duncombepark.com. The National Centre for Birds of Prey is another attraction in the grounds, tel 0844 7422035 www.ncbp.co.uk.

HELMSLEY CASTLE

Not every visitor to Helmsley is aware of Helmsley Castle, despite its proximity to the town centre. It was built around 1200 and saw plenty of strife in 1644, during the Civil War. Colonel Crosland held the castle for the Crown, while Sir Thomas Fairfax led the besieging Parliamentarian force. Fairfax was hit by a musket ball during one assault, and his siege was threatened by a Royalist relief force from Knaresborough Castle. The relief force was eventually beaten back and harried as far as Black Hambleton. The castle surrendered towards the end of 1644 and was rendered useless during 1646 and 1647 when parts of the keep and walls were destroyed. The castle is managed by English Heritage and there is an entrance charge, tel 01439 770442.

The ruined Helmsley Castle keep was sleighted by Cromwellian forces

WALK 10
Hawnby Hill and Easterside Hill

Start/finish	The Inn at Hawnby, Hawnby, SE 542 898
Distance	7.5km (4½ miles)
Total ascent/descent	330m (1080ft)
Time	2hrs 30mins
Terrain	A short but sometimes difficult walk, as paths can be steep and rugged; paths clear at first, but later covered in bracken
Maps	OS Landranger 100; OS Explorer OL26 South
Refreshments	The Inn at Hawnby in the village of Hawnby
Transport	None to Hawnby, but summer weekend Moorsbus services between Helmsley and Bilsdale pass Laskill, which is close to Easterside Hill

Rising from the confluence of Ryedale and Bilsdale, Hawnby Hill and Easterside Hill are twins with a striking appearance, flanked by gentle dales and gently sloping heather moors. But for the fact they sit lower than the surrounding moorlands, they would command attention from afar, but despite their steep slopes and shapely form, visitors tend to notice them only at close quarters. This walk uses a variety of paths to traverse the crest of Hawnby Hill and climb near the summit of Easterside Hill in a fine, short circular walk from the charming little village of Hawnby.

Hawnby is only a small village and the Inn at Hawnby stands at a road junction from where a public footpath is signposted uphill. Climb up an old lane to reach a gate where paths are marked left and right. Take the left path, but not up to the step-stile as marked. Instead, go a little further uphill to a small gate in the top corner of a field. Go through the gate and follow a narrow path that swings right and climbs steeply up a slope of bracken, becoming a clear, grassy path on the crest of Hawnby Hill. The summit cairn is reached at 294m (965ft), and there are extensive views across Ryedale to Black Hambleton,

across Bilsdale Moor and Bransdale Moor, to neighbouring Easterside Hill, and the distant Yorkshire Wolds.

Continue along a sharper part of the crest, where bouldery limestone scree falls to the left. Keep straight ahead along the ridge, then zigzag down the steep end of the hill, aiming for a cattle grid on a road at **Moor Gate**. Cross the grid and turn right along a gravel access road across a moorland slope. Go down to a gate, before reaching **Sportsman's Hall**, and turn left alongside a wall. Turn right into a field and keep left as if heading up through a valley, then follow a wet and muddy path down into woodland to cross a footbridge over **Ladhill Beck**.

The path leading uphill is a little vague, but it becomes clearer as it climbs a boulder-strewn moorland slope. Cross a grassy track on the heather and bilberry slope and go over a stone step-stile at the top corner of a wall. Continue across the heather moor, as marked

The striking profile of Hawnby Hill as seen from the upper part of Ryedale

by paint blobs and small cairns. Follow a wall onwards and forge through bracken as the wall turns right across a slope. Watch carefully for a waymark arrow and a stile on the right, pointing uphill to indicate an old path on the hillside. Follow this faithfully uphill, noting marker posts across the higher slopes of Easterside Hill, at over 280m (920ft). Watch for more marker posts on the descent, then cross a field to land on a minor road at **Easterside Farm** B&B. Turn right to follow the road downhill, then more steeply downhill to cross Ladhill Beck. A steep climb up the road is followed by a left turn at the top to return to the village of **Hawnby**.

THE HAMBLETON HILLS

The view across country towards Bilsdale Moor as seen from Hawnby Hill (Walk 10)

THE HAMBLETON HILLS

Geologically, the Hambleton Hills are an extension of the Tabular Hills, separated by Ryedale, and with a character all of their own. Essentially, the Hambleton Hills rise gently from the dales within the North York Moors National Park, then drop precipitously to the plains. Indeed, some of the slopes are not only steep, but excessively steep and may even have cliff edges. Despite having the appearance of an inaccessible rampart, these cliffs are breached by a busy main road at Sutton Bank, along which many visitors find their way into the national park. To catch visitors at an appropriate point, the national park authority constructed a visitor centre at the top of this road.

Many walkers have come to know and love the Hambleton Hills by setting off along the waymarked Cleveland Way, one of Britain's national trails. This route leads from Helmsley to Rievaulx, then climbs gradually from the dales via the village of Cold Kirby to reach Sutton Bank. At that point walkers are faced with a choice of routes, as there is a diversion to see the celebrated Kilburn White Horse, which was carved into the steep slopes in the 19th century. However, it is the cliff-edge walk that is the most memorable feature of these hills, and when the cliffs finally give way to mere hillsides, the course of the ancient Hambleton Drove Road is another abiding feature. This long, straight track soars over the moors, almost reaching the summit of Black Hambleton itself.

There is no doubt that by the time walkers experience the broad heather slopes of Black Hambleton, comparisons with the High Moors in the central parts of the national park are inevitable. Black Hambleton is both high and heathery enough to rival most of the broad bleak moors at the heart of the North York Moors, and many walkers crossing its flanks will find themselves yearning for more of the same.

Four walks in the Hambleton Hills are described, showcasing some of the variety of the landscapes in this little limestone upland. Rievaulx Abbey and Byland Abbey are visited on separate walks and have obvious monastic links. The splendid cliff-edge walk from Sutton Bank is complemented by an exploration of the lower slopes around curious Gormire Lake. A longer walk takes in a few villages before heading for the high and wild slopes of Black Hambleton, by which time the High Moors and Cleveland Hills begin to dominate onward views and altogether tougher walks begin to beckon.

Cliffs drop steeply from Sutton Bank to wooded slopes below (Walk 13)

WALK 11
Rievaulx Abbey and Old Byland

Start/finish	Rievaulx Abbey, SE 574 848
Distance	10.75km (6¾ miles)
Total ascent/descent	160m (525ft)
Time	3hrs 30mins
Terrain	Generally easy walking along minor roads, clear tracks and paths, although some paths can be a bit overgrown or muddy
Maps	OS Landranger 100; OS Explorer OL26 South
Refreshments	Tearoom at Rievaulx Abbey
Transport	Summer weekend Moorsbus services link Helmsley and Rievaulx Abbey

Rievaulx Abbey is a remarkable sight, its stout soaring columns and elegant arches dominating the small stone village of Rievaulx. Naturally the abbey attracts a lot of visitors, and the nearby Cleveland Way is quite popular too, but some of the other paths and tracks in the area, such as those around the village of Old Byland, are much quieter. This walk is essentially confined to wooded dales, except when it crosses higher fields to get from one dale to another. Allow plenty of extra time if exploring Rievaulx Abbey or Rievaulx Terrace.

A tearoom and toilets are available, as well as parking for patrons.

Start at Rievaulx Abbey, either exploring the site straight away or taking note of its opening times for later in the day. ◄ Parking is tight around Rievaulx, and on summer weekends it is best to use the Moorsbus for access. Walk along a road beside the River Rye to reach **Rievaulx Bridge**. Turn right to cross it and walk straight ahead to pass a road junction, following the road signposted for Scawton until a clear gravel track on the right is marked as the Cleveland Way.

The track runs alongside a wood and passes a few shallow fishing ponds, then the route crosses stepping

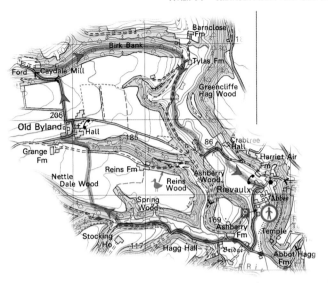

stones on the right. Go through a small gate, cross a track, cross a step-stile, cross a small field and cross a footbridge – all in that order. Turn left uphill through **Nettle Dale Wood** and keep to the trodden path that climbs gradually uphill (don't take the path that branches left). Emerge to walk alongside fields and go through gates, crossing a track, before going through another gate into a wood. Turn left along a path lined with nettles and brambles to pass through a little wooded dale, gradually crossing the valley before being drawn up to a small gate. Step on to a road and turn right to enter the village of **Old Byland**, following the road as it swings left to reach a sloping green surrounded by old stone houses.

Walk to the top end of the village and turn left as signposted for Hawnby and Boltby, then turn right at a junction. Walk straight along a narrow road marked as leading to a ford. The road swings left and drops into Caydale, overlooking **Caydale Mill**. Before reaching the bottom of the road, watch for a sharp right turn at a gate signposted as a public bridleway. Follow a grassy path

OLD BYLAND

The village of Old Byland is indeed old, having been mentioned in the Domesday Book as 'Begesland'. The village had a wooden church at the time, but there might have been a stone church on the site previously. The land around Old Byland was granted to Savignian monks in 1142, who created the layout of the village that we see today. They left soon afterwards, in 1147, to build Byland Abbey, which is seen on Walk 12. Visitors would miss All Saints Church if it wasn't signposted, and careful study of its stonework reveals some interesting Norman carvings.

across a flowery, grassy slope. The path runs almost down to a river, then rises to enter a coppice woodland. The path in the woods can be quite muddy, and it later runs across a slope at **Birk Bank**, where conifers have been felled. Continue back into deciduous woodland as the path drops gradually downhill. Go through a gate and along a grassy track, then through another gate on to a tarmac farm road near **Tylas Farm**.

Turn right along the road and follow it down into a dip. Turn left to leave the road at a gate and follow a clear path through a field. Continue along a duckboard path on a wooded slope above the River Rye. Cross a stile and continue across a rough strip of land to reach a track. Turn left to follow the track over the fine stone arch of Bow Bridge. Walk uphill until you see a footpath signpost and a small gate on the right. Follow a riverside path downstream as marked. ◀ Keep going through gates to reach a road in the village of **Rievaulx** and turn right to return to the abbey.

A muddy ditch off to the left is an old canal that was used to float stone to Rievaulx Abbey during its construction.

Founded in 1132 by Walter l'Espec, **Rievaulx Abbey** was a Cistercian house and once the home of St Aelred. During its construction a short canal was built, and rafts bore blocks of stone to the site. The abbey is built almost on a north–south axis, rather than the usual east–west axis, because it is situated in a rather narrow dale. Only 35 years after its foundation the abbey boasted 140 monks, 250 lay

brothers and 260 hired laymen. Even in its ruinous state the walls rise to a prodigious height, giving a good impression of the size and complexity of the building. The abbey is managed by English Heritage and there is an entrance charge, tel 01439 798228.

Rievaulx Abbey in its secluded wooded valley

An optional short extension involves turning left along the road in Rievaulx and walking through the village to pass the church. Here, look out on the right for a path winding up a wooded slope to **Rievaulx Terrace and Temples**, a National Trust property.

RIEVAULX TERRACE AND TEMPLES

The grassy brow of Rievaulx Terrace offers fine views and a short extension to the day's walk. There are two classical temples: the Tuscan Temple and the Ionic Temple. Both were built in the 18th century and the Ionic Temple features splendid paintings on its ceiling. There is an entrance charge, tel 01439 748203.

WALK 12

Byland Abbey, Mount Snever and Oldstead

Start/finish	Abbey Inn, Byland Abbey, SE 548 789
Distance	7.5km (4½ miles)
Total ascent/descent	200m (655ft)
Time	2hrs 30mins
Terrain	Easy walking along field paths and farm tracks, although some woodland paths are overgrown
Maps	OS Landranger 100; OS Explorer OL26 South
Refreshments	Abbey Inn Tearoom at Byland Abbey, Stapylton Arms at Wass, Black Swan Inn at Oldstead
Transport	Transdev buses serve Byland Abbey from Helmsley and York, and there are summer Sunday Moorsbus services from Helmsley

Byland Abbey's west wall is an outstanding feature seen in many pictorial compilations of scenes from the North York Moors. The top half of its round window has collapsed, leaving two horns of masonry pointing up towards the sky. The nearby villages of Wass and Oldstead are pretty, but lack any outstanding features, although both offer refreshments. Mount Snever is no more than a wooded hill, and the Mount Snever Observatory is a curious viewpoint tower. However, a gentle circular walk taking in all these places opens up a quiet and interesting part of the national park to visitors.

Start at the Abbey Inn Tearoom and admire Byland Abbey. Follow the road signposted for Wass, then turn left along the Abbey House access road. Don't walk to the house, but turn right and cross stiles through rather wet fields, bearing a little to the left uphill to find a small gate. The path passes through an orchard to reach a road just outside the village of **Wass**. Turn left up a battered woodland road, and go straight through a little gate signposted for Cam Farm to follow a grassy path beside a wood. The path climbs to a stile and enters the wood at a pronounced bend on a track. Head left as signposted again for Cam Farm. The track dips downhill, then rises, then swings sharp left. Keep right at this point, in effect walking straight ahead, to follow another track. As this track climbs it can be a bit muddy, and it narrows to become a brambly path at a higher level around **Elm Hag**.

Emerge on to a track and turn right to follow it to the edge of the woods, reaching a gate. Don't leave the woods, but turn left along a grassy path just inside them. Turn left into a birch wood, where the bracken tends to obscure the path. ▸ Eventually, you will reach **Mount Snevers Observatory** – a stout stone tower built as a viewpoint in 1888; however, it is generally locked with no access. You can read the verses and inscriptions carved on the walls, and wonder what the view might be like without the trees!

A path drops steeply from the tower through **Snever Wood**. Follow it all the way down to a track, and turn right to follow the track, which continues more gently downhill. Keep left at track junctions to leave the woods and follow a narrow tarmac road downhill. Keep left at road junctions to follow the road just as far as the first buildings in the village of **Oldstead**. ▸ However, to continue the walk turn left along an access road to pass gate piers, as if heading for Oldstead Mill, along a tree-shaded avenue.

A footpath signpost points uphill to the right, then you turn left along the top of a wooded brow. Walk alongside small fields, using stiles and gates, then follow the path down to a minor road. Turn right, as if walking back towards the village of Oldstead, but turn left along the access road for **Oldstead Grange**. Pass in front of a farm guesthouse and walk through the farmyard.

Note the rugged, jumbled earthworks of Camp Holes to the left.

If you enter the village you will find the Black Swan Inn at the far end.

The Black Swan Inn at Oldstead, where a short detour leads to food and drink

Cross a stile beside a gate as marked. Walk down a grassy track into a valley and cross a stile beside a gate at the bottom. Turn left up a narrow path through a tangled belt of woodland. Keep right, and then turn left to follow a field boundary, keeping well clear of the farmhouse at **Cams Head**. Switch to another field boundary as marked and signposted for Byland Abbey to continue. The path heads diagonally across a field, then runs alongside an orchard to cross a stile and reach a road. Turn left along the road to return to **Byland Abbey** and the Abbey Inn Tearoom.

BYLAND ABBEY

After rejecting a site at Old Byland (see Walk 11), the Savignian monks chose to found an abbey here, although they had to drain the land before building in 1177. The ruins of Byland Abbey are quite extensive, but rather dominated by what you see from the roadside. In fact the abbey extended far beyond what can be discerned on the ground, and was larger than Rievaulx and Fountains abbeys. A fine spread of decorative floor tiles remain in their original position. The abbey grounds had fish ponds, a mill and market gardens, so that it was entirely self-sufficient for food. The abbey is managed by English Heritage and there is an entrance charge, tel 01347 868614.

Byland Abbey once covered a larger area than the current ruins

WALK 13
Sutton Bank, Gormire Lake and the White Horse

Start/finish	National Park Centre, Sutton Bank, SE 515 830
Distance	13.5km (8½ miles)
Total ascent/descent	310m (1015ft)
Time	4hrs 45mins
Terrain	Generally easy paths along cliff edges and through forest, woods and fields, as well as farm and forest tracks; some paths might be overgrown.
Maps	OS Landranger 100; OS Explorer OL26 South
Refreshments	Restaurant at the visitor centre on Sutton Bank; the Forresters Arms is off-route at Kilburn.
Transport	Summer Sunday Moorsbus services link Helmsley and Sutton Bank.

The most dramatic part of the Hambleton Hills is around Sutton Bank, where cliff edges and steep, wooded slopes face west towards the plains. The Cleveland Way makes use of the cliff-top paths, but walkers on that route know little of what lies at the foot of the slope. This walk reveals a network of paths and tracks, reaches the shore of Gormire Lake and wanders past farms and through woods to climb to the Kilburn White Horse. All this is achieved from Sutton Bank, one of the gateways to the North York Moors National Park, where there is an interesting and informative visitor centre.

Leave the National Park Centre at Sutton Bank and walk as if you are going to follow the busy A170 road over the edge. However, turn right to follow the path signposted as the Cleveland Way. The path initially runs through patchy woodland for around 300m (985ft), with only occasional glimpses over the cliffs to the left. Gormire Lake can be seen in a wooded hollow at the foot of **Whitestone Cliff**, with the plains stretching beyond. The cliff path is grassy and gently graded, dropping slightly as it turns right and later swings left in the Garbutt Wood Nature Reserve. The cliffs become a wooded slope at **South Woods**, before you begin a gradual ascent towards **Boltby Scar**; however, our route turns left downhill beforehand, signposted as a bridleway to Boltby. ▸

The path runs down a grassy groove, then a gate leads into a forest. Follow a muddy track downhill and cross a forest track. Go through a gate and cross the open space of **Little Moor**. Pass through another gate and follow a forest path further downhill. The forest gives way to oak and birch, before providing views across lower fields. Turn left and follow a path downhill, just inside the woodland, towards Greendale, and go through a gate to approach the farm.

Just before reaching the buildings, turn left and cross a stile to follow a narrow path rising across a slope of bracken. Watch carefully for the line of the path, and more markers, to cross a rugged, overgrown slope of bracken and brambles between a forest and a wood to reach a field beyond. Leave the field through a gate and pick a way through thistles, while keeping well to the left of **Southwoods Hall**. Go through another gate and swing right alongside the stout fence encircling the hall. A bridleway signpost points through a small gate marked with a blue arrow. Join and follow the access road a short way from the hall, then walk parallel to the road in an adjacent field, as directed, to pass the main gate. Walk straight ahead through another gate and follow a track straight ahead. At the end, go through a gate beside a house and turn left, then

Looking ahead, contorted larches cover the site of an Iron Age hill fort.

A path signposted straight uphill offers an early return to Sutton Bank.

swing right into wild woodlands to reach the shore of **Gormire Lake**. ◀

> **Gormire Lake** is entirely natural, but unusual, since the area does not readily support lakes. It was formed when a huge section of the escarpment slumped on to the plains, so that the detached strata tilted back at an angle, leaving a small valley between itself and the freshly broken cliff face. The valley was filled with rubble and clay from the fracture, so that water was able to pool in a hollow, whereas normally it would have seeped into the limestone bedrock. According to local lore the lake is bottomless – in fact it is quite shallow. The surrounding woodlands are home to red, fallow and roe deer, although these are seldom seen.

Follow the woodland path away from the shore and go through a gate to reach Gormire Farm. Turn right into the farmyard, then left to leave through a gate. Continue as marked along a grassy track to another gate. Keep right to walk up through a field and cross a step-stile. Walk down through a field to reach a gate and step-stile that give way to the busy **A170** road. Turn right to walk alongside the road, then cross it to find a step-stile in a hedge.

Walk down from the busy road towards **Hood Grange** and keep to the right of the farm buildings. Cross the access road and a small footbridge beyond. Turn left as directed alongside a field, then turn right as signposted up through a big field to enter a forest at a corner. Turn left up a forest track, which later dips downhill a little. Keep straight on at a junction, up and over a forested gap between **Hood Hill** and Roulston Scar. Walk downhill and keep left at a junction to follow a track that climbs through a mixed plantation. Turn right at a junction and contour to reach a barrier gate and minor road. Cross the road and turn left up a path on the steep wooded slope. Cross back over the road to follow a clear path to reach the celebrated **White Horse**, although it is difficult to see from such close quarters.

Gormire Lake fills a wooded hollow below a limestone cliff face

Only the head of the **White Horse** can be seen from the path. It was cut in 1857 under the direction of local schoolmaster John Hodgson. The inspiration came from another local man, Thomas Taylor, who had witnessed the cleaning and maintenance of a white horse in the south. As the bedrock is oolitic limestone, rather than white chalk, the Kilburn White Horse needs occasional applications of whitewash. The figure measures 96m (314ft) by 69m (228ft) and is a landmark for many on the lower plains. Of greater antiquity, cutting across a nearby glider field, is the Casten Dike, which may have once formed a defensive or territorial boundary on the promontory.

Follow a clear path along a cliff edge of **Roulston Scar**, at around 290m (950ft). There is a small airfield here, so heed the warning signs: do not make a short-cut

The view back along the cliffs from Sutton Bank at the end of the walk

Author James Herriot had a special affection for the view from here.

across the airfield, watch out for low-flying aircraft and do not tamper with towing cables. Later, pass a three-fingered signpost for the Cleveland Way, and stay on the clearest cliff-edge path as signposted for **Sutton Bank**. ◀ Cross the busy A170 and keep to the right, through a car park, to return to the National Park Centre.

The **North York Moors National Park Centre** catches tourists at one of the busiest entry points for the national park. Displays and exhibits focus on conservation to encourage sensitive and thoughtful recreation. Maps and guides are on sale, and there is a restaurant and toilets on site. Summer Sunday Moorsbus services link the centre with Helmsley, to encourage visitors to leave their cars behind. To check opening times, tel 01845 597426.

WALK 14

Osmotherley, Thimbleby, Siltons
and Black Hambleton

Start/finish	Market Cross, Osmotherley, SE 456 972
Distance	18km (11 miles)
Total ascent/descent	460m (1510ft)
Time	6hrs
Terrain	Generally easy, but a long walk with field paths, forest tracks, minor roads and farm tracks, followed by a high moorland track
Maps	OS Landrangers 99 and 100; OS Explorer OL26 South
Refreshments	Queen Catherine Hotel, Golden Lion, restaurant and tearooms in Osmotherley; Gold Cup Inn at Nether Silton
Transport	Regular Abbott's bus services to Osmotherley from Northallerton and Stokesley

The Hambleton Hills reach their highest and proudest moment on Black Hambleton – a moorland crest so wild and heathery that it rivals the High Moors stretching westwards. The Hambleton Drove Road has long been regarded as a classic route over the broad moorland top, and the Cleveland Way makes good use of it between Sutton Bank and Osmotherley. Few walkers know their way around the lower slopes, yet there are lovely little villages that can be linked with roads, tracks and paths; there are also forests, fields and farms to explore. All this can be achieved on the following walk.

Start at the Market Cross in Osmotherley and follow the Stokesley road a short way. Turn left along School Lane and go straight down a narrow, enclosed path, continuing straight down a field where trees create a low-headroom situation! Go through a gate at the bottom and turn right along a track, which becomes grassy, then cross a metal footbridge over **Cod Beck**. Walk through a field and cross an access track, then pass a sports pitch where the path is overgrown. Continue beside a field to reach a minor road near **Home Farm**. Turn right along the road, up into the village of **Thimbleby** and out the other side.

Turn left where an old sign reads, 'Bridle Road and Footpath to Siltons'. Walk up a broad clear track and go into a forest. Turn right, as marked, then at a fork head up to the left as marked. Follow the forest track uphill, crossing bare rock at times, before it swings left at the top, at around 230m (755ft). Turn right down a narrow woodland path, which is steep and runs through a slippery runnel,

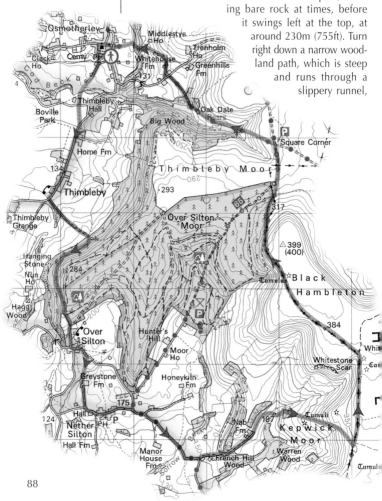

before landing on a narrow road. Turn right to follow the road down into the village of **Over Silton**.

Turn left at a junction and follow the road signposted for **Nether Silton**. Watch out for a gate, stile and bridleway signpost on the right. Walk down through a field, through a gate and across a beck. Walk up to **Greystone Farm** and leave along its access track. Turn left up a road into Nether Silton, passing its sloping green and the Gold Cup Inn. Follow the road up out of the village, then downhill as signposted for **Kepwick**. The huge bulk of Black Hambleton rises to the left and will be reached in due course, but first cross a bridge at the bottom of the road, then follow the road uphill and turn left to reach Cross Lodge.

Turn left at the lodge to follow a farm access road uphill; this passes between a pine-clad hill and a wooded valley. Keep to the right of the buildings at **Nab Farm** to follow a clear track onwards. The track swings right to cross a stream, after which you turn left up through a gate in a wall. An obvious grassy path leads up a bracken slope on to heathery **Kepwick Moor**, then follows a drystone wall over a grassy moor to reach a gate. Go through the gate to find more heather and turn left to follow the Hambleton Drove Road.

Turn left along a broad track with a drystone wall to the left. Go through a gate on to a heather moor and enjoy views across to the distant Yorkshire Dales. Watch

HAMBLETON DROVE ROAD

This ancient drove road may have been based on a prehistoric ridgeway. Travellers and traders would have found it easier to traverse the high ground than risk passage through the plains, which were densely wooded, swampy in places and inhabited by wild animals. Even long after the lowlands were tamed, cattle drovers used the high ground to avoid enclosed farmland and expensive turnpikes. Drovers covered immense distances, moving livestock from Scotland to London for a good price when stock was scarce around the capital. The 18th and 19th centuries saw brisk trade, with herds of up to 1000 on the move. As drovers could be charged 1s/6d (7½p) per score of cattle on a turnpike, great savings were made by avoiding them!

A view of the little reservoir and surrounding woodlands in Oak Dale

out for a left turn after a cattle grid at **Whitestones**, where the old drove road, still accompanied by the wall, rises gently across the slopes of **Black Hambleton**. The track reaches an altitude of 390m (1280ft), while the highest point on the moorland, at 399m (1309ft), is close to hand and easily visited by a short detour.

If the day is clear, the descent along the track includes a view of Osmotherley, although this will be lost later. Walk alongside a forest to reach the signposted **Square Corner** on a minor road on Thimbleby Moor. Turn left to follow a stone-pitched path down into a wooded dale. Cross a footbridge over a stream and follow a reservoir access road past a house called **Oak Dale**, heading downhill to cross a bridge before climbing uphill through woods.

Turn left down a minor road, then right up a track. Turn left downhill, towards **Whitehouse Farm**, but keep well to the right along a path and walk down to a footbridge spanning a stream. Climb flights of stone steps on a wooded slope and follow a clear path through fields to reach **Osmotherley**. Simply walk straight ahead, quietly, along a narrow alleyway to reach the Market Cross on the green where the walk started.

A flagstone path leads through fields on the way to Osmotherley

THE CLEVELAND HILLS

*A gateway is passed above a grassy gap between
Hasty Bank and Cold Moor (Walk 17)*

THE CLEVELAND HILLS

The Cleveland Hills are memorable for their shapely forms and steepness. In a sense they are simply a continuation of the west-facing scarp that looks out from the North York Moors to the level plains. However, the scarp slope is cut deeply by rugged gaps and valleys that leave outstanding little hills with fairly distinctive shapes, quite unlike the rolling tablelands and moorlands that are common in other parts of the national park. In effect, walkers traversing this little range find themselves on a monstrous roller coaster, climbing steeply uphill, enjoying high-level promenades, then dropping steeply to rugged gaps between the hills, over and over again.

The underlying rocks in this range are essentially from the Lower and Middle Jurassic period, some 170–200 million years old. The lower beds include Lias shales and ironstones, which have been extensively quarried, while the neighbouring High Moors are generally capped by sandstones from the Ravenscar Group, which is why the moorlands present smoother profiles than the dissected Cleveland Hills at the edge of the North York Moors. Over the past few centuries these hills were hacked and blasted by quarrymen and miners in search of alum shales, ironstone and jet, leaving some slopes looking bare and barren, while other places are covered in rocky rubble.

Over the past few decades the Cleveland Way, Lyke Wake Walk, Coast to Coast Walk and other less well-known routes have been drawn along the crest of the Cleveland Hills, so that countless thousands of walkers have experienced the delights, as well as the rigours, of the full traverse. With the sheer pressure of pounding feet, huge scars were ripped out of the hillsides, so that extensive restoration had to take place. Walkers who remember the days when the hills were scored by trenches full of mud and rubble will now be amazed to find stone-paved paths with re-vegetated margins, which have the potential to last for centuries with a little ongoing care and maintenance.

Five walks are offered in the following pages to enable walkers to explore the Cleveland Hills. One of them is a fairly gentle walk over Beacon Hill from Osmotherley. Two rather more strenuous walks climb into the hills from Chop Gate at the head of Bilsdale. Another two moderate walks explore lesser-known parts of the range from the tiny little village of Kildale. Bear in mind that the course of the Lyke Wake Walk, described towards the end of this guidebook, offers another chance to enjoy an extended day's walk through the Cleveland Hills. The true scale and nature of the range quickly becomes apparent as each splendid hill is climbed in turn, and then you climb another!

WALK 15

Osmotherley, Beacon Hill and High Lane

Start/finish	Market Cross, Osmotherley, SE 456 972
Distance	13km (8 miles), or 9.5km (6 miles) without detours
Total ascent/descent	390m (1280ft), or 260m (855ft) without detours
Time	4hrs or 3hrs without detours
Terrain	Generally easy paths and tracks through fields, with some woodland, moorland and short, steep slopes
Maps	OS Landrangers 93, 99 and 100; OS Explorer OL26 South and North
Refreshments	Queen Catherine Hotel, Golden Lion, restaurant and tearooms in Osmotherley
Transport	Regular Abbott's bus services to Osmotherley from Northallerton and Stokesley

Beacon Hill is the most accessible and gentle of the Cleveland Hills. From its summit there are good views of the bleaker parts of the North York Moors National Park. The hill is easily climbed from Osmotherley, and as this is a short walk, there is scope for making detours to interesting places such as Lady's Chapel and Mount Grace Priory. Later on the walk takes in a fine old track called High Lane, which runs closer to the moors, before it incorporates a short stretch of the Cleveland Way to return straight to Osmotherley.

Leave the Market Cross in Osmotherley by following the road called North End. Pass a pinfold, where stray animals were once impounded. Turn left near the top of the village as signposted for the Cleveland Way, along Ruebury Lane. Follow this access road as it climbs past a few houses, continuing uphill along a track to reach a fork. The **Lady's Chapel** is signposted up to the right and is reached by following a track flanked by the Stations of the Cross.

This **old chapel**, attached to a house and restored from a ruin, is said to have been built in 1515 by Catherine of Aragon, first wife of Henry VIII, for the recluse Thomas Parkinson. A number of miracles are said to have taken place there, and the chapel remains a popular site of pilgrimage.

Walk back down the access track and turn right as signposted for the Cleveland Way. When you reach **Chapel Wood Farm**, turn left to walk through the farmyard, then walk into fields and turn right downhill as directed. Cross a stile at the bottom corner of the fields, then walk down a path through **Mount Grace Wood**. A footbridge finally leads to a car park, where there is access to **Mount Grace Priory** ruins, the Jacobean manor and its lovely gardens.

Mount Grace Priory was a Carthusian monastery founded in 1398 by Thomas de Holand. Of particular interest are the two-storey monks' cells around the cloister, one of which has been restored to its original condition. Each cell had a living room, study, bedroom and small herb garden. The central tower of the priory church remains intact. The ruins stand beside an interesting

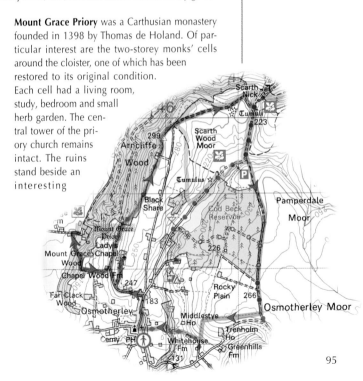

Jacobean manor, and there are lovely gardens to explore. The priory is owned by the National Trust and managed by English Heritage, and there is an entrance charge, tel 01609 883494.

Retrace your steps back up to Chapel Wood Farm and walk through the farmyard before turning left to follow a track away from the farm. Go through a gate into **Arncliffe Wood**. Turn right up a clear path and continue along the inside edge of the wood, following a drystone wall over the crest of the hill. Pass the British Telecom station on Beacon Hill, as well as a trig point at 299m (981ft), then drop downhill to reach a couple of gates leading on to heathery **Scarth Wood Moor**. ◀ A clear, paved path runs down the moorland slope. Turn right at a junction to walk down a track signposted as a bridleway – this leads to a minor road at **Scarth Nick**.

Scarth Nick was cut by glacial melt-water when a torrent poured through a gap in the hills as a stagnant mass of ice melted on the higher ground. The road at Scarth Nick is quite innocuous, but in the 18th century the well-travelled Arthur Young was

Views ahead through the Cleveland Hills lead the eye to the little pyramidal peak of Roseberry Topping, seen in the distance.

A stone-paved path leads across Scarth Wood Moor towards Scarth Nick

scathing about it. He said, 'The going down into Cleveland is beyond all description terrible ... for you go through such steep, rough, narrow, rocky precipices that I would sincerely advise any friend to go a hundred miles to avoid it.'

Turn right to walk up the road, crossing its highest part and walking downhill. Turn left across a footbridge by a ford and walk up a steep and rocky track. The rest of this track, called High Lane, is gently graded and easy. As the track rises on to **Pamperdale Moor** there is forest to the right and rough enclosed pastures on the left. The highest parts run at 270m (885ft), and the track eventually becomes a tarmac road on Osmotherley Moor. Turn right as signposted along a public footpath and walk along a grassy track on a brow at Rookhaw. Views across a valley take in the moorland hump of Black Hambleton.

Cross a stile at the end of the track and walk alongside a field. Walk down alongside another field to cross a horse gallop and reach another track. Turn left to follow the track downhill as it narrows, flanked by bushes. Turn right as signposted for the Cleveland Way and walk down towards **Whitehouse Farm**, but keep well to the right of it along a path. Walk down to a footbridge spanning a stream, then climb flights of stone steps on a wooded slope and follow a clear path through fields to reach **Osmotherley**. Simply walk straight ahead, quietly, along a narrow alleyway to reach the Market Cross on the green where the walk started.

OSMOTHERLEY

Osmotherley was once known as 'Asmundrelac', or 'Asmund's clearing'. It is a charming stone village with a green heart. Three roads meet at the Market Cross, and there is a stone table on five legs where baskets of market produce were sold. John Wesley preached from this stone, and the Methodist chapel in the village has a date-stone of 1754. There is accommodation, including a youth hostel and campsite, the Queen Catherine and Golden Lion pubs, restaurant, tearoom, fish and chip shop, village store, bus services and toilets.

WALK 16
Chop Gate, Cringle Moor and Cock Howe

Start/finish	Chop Gate car park, Bilsdale, SE 558 993
Distance	15.5km (9½ miles)
Total ascent/descent	540m (1770ft)
Time	5hrs
Terrain	A tough walk along firm, clear paths and tracks, although these can be muddy for short stretches; the high moors are exposed in bad weather
Maps	OS Landrangers 93 and 100; OS Explorer OL26 South and North
Refreshments	Buck Inn at Chop Gate, Lordstones Café at Carlton Bank
Transport	Summer weekend Moorsbus services link Chop Gate with Helmsley, Stokesley and Guisborough

Cringle Moor is undoubtedly one of the finest of the Cleveland Hills, its steep northern slopes looking northwards across the plains, while neighbouring hills rise close on either side. Walkers usually climb it from the Lordstones Café on Carlton Bank in mere minutes, but the route offered here is a fine day's walk from Chop Gate (pronounced Chop 'Yat') in Bilsdale. The route follows the crest of Cold Moor, then after crossing a gap, it climbs up Cringle Moor on a steep and stony path. After providing fine views, the route descends to Lord Stones Café, where you can take a break. It then traverses the moorlands on the western side of Bilsdale. Barker's Ridge leads to Noon Hill, where a direct descent leads to Chop Gate.

Leave the car park at Chop Gate and follow the road up through the little village, passing the Buck Inn. Turn left at a road junction, then almost immediately right up a short cobbled road to a Methodist chapel. Go straight up a narrow, enclosed and sometimes muddy path. This becomes a fine grassy track later, passing through gates while climbing between fields. There is another rugged stretch along the track before a gate gives way to an open moor.

Drift to the right and follow a wall up to a forest, then drift to the left up a moorland path that can be rugged in places. Join and follow a clear track along the crest of the moorland, passing the heather humps of **tumuli** on Three Howes. Cross a dip, then follow a clear but narrow path past a cairn on the crest. Keep to the crest to reach the summit of **Cold Moor** at 401m (1316ft).

The Cleveland Way is joined at this point, so turn left to follow it as a stone-paved path straight down to a gap. Go through a gate as marked and reach an area of shale spoil. Go through another gate, then the path uphill is steep, equipped with lots of little zigzags to ease the gradient a little. Eventually the slope begins to level out and a fine path curves round the abrupt northern edge of **Cringle Moor** around 420m (1380ft).

Follow the stone-paved or firm gritty path around the edge, then descend a little to reach a stone **viewpoint** seat dedicated to local rambler Alec Falconer at Cringle End. Turn left to continue the descent, using a stone-paved path running close to a drystone wall. Go through a gate at the bottom and walk along a grassy track flanked by a wall and a fence. Walk across a grassy area and bear in mind that there is immediate access to

Looking along the path from Cringle Moor to Lord Stones and Carlton Bank

Lord Stones Café, a shop and toilets in a car park surrounded by trees.

Cross a minor road and follow the stone-paved Cleveland Way up a bracken slope on **Carlton Bank**, but turn left and leave it to follow a track through a gate. Continue uphill until the track makes a pronounced bend to the right, at which point you leave it using a narrow path on the left, signposted as a bridleway. The path forges through heather to reach a track. Turn left at a nearby junction and the track is broad and clear as it meanders around the moorland crest. Skirt round a rocky rash and later descend to the rushy pool of Brian's Pond.

Keep straight ahead at a junction, along a broad path signposted as a footpath, which later narrows. It swings to the right of the moorland crest and enjoys views down into Scugdale. Pass **Barker's Crags**, then cross a stile and head back on to the heathery moorland crest as marked. There is a junction of paths and tracks, but simply walk straight ahead to climb gently up the clearest track in view, going through a gate to continue up a moorland crest.

The broad, stony track is roughly aligned to the crest, and the towering mast of the Bilsdale transmitter is in view ahead. ▶ Looking back, note how the shapely form of Roseberry Topping seems to sail past the gap between Cringle Moor and Cold Moor. Turn left at a track junction and rise gently. Look out for a stone upright pierced by a hole on **Green Howe** at 404m (1325ft). Keep to the track, but turn left later to reach another stone upright and cairn on **Cock Howe**.

The mast is 314m (1030ft) tall.

Follow a narrow path onwards down a heather slope into Bilsdale. This is clear enough, and while it is augmented by blobs of paint, it is quite rugged in parts. Walk down the heather moor, then go straight down a steep and slippery slope of crumbling shale covered in bracken. Avoid a grooved path bending to the right. Cross a step-stile and continue down through fields, entering a deep-cut groove later. Land on a track finally cross a wooden bridge over **Raisdale Beck** to return to the car park and toilets at **Chop Gate**.

WALK 17

Chop Gate, Urra Moor, Hasty Bank and Cold Moor

Start/finish	Chop Gate car park, Bilsdale, SE 558 993
Distance	14km (8¾ miles)
Total ascent/descent	540m (1770ft)
Time	5hrs
Terrain	A tough walk along clear paths and tracks, although these can be muddy for short stretches; the high moors are exposed in bad weather
Maps	OS Landrangers 93 and 100; OS Explorer OL26 South and North
Refreshments	Buck Inn at Chop Gate
Transport	Summer weekend Moorsbus services link Chop Gate and Clay Bank with Helmsley, Stokesley and Guisborough

The hills grouped around the head of Bilsdale offer a fine day's walk, and the tiny village of Chop Gate is a good starting point. A clear path and track offer an easy approach to Urra Moor, where Round Hill is the highest point in the North York Moors National Park. The course of the Cleveland Way can be followed down to a road on Clay Bank from where a steep climb leads on to the level top of Hasty Bank. The aggressive, chunky blocks known as the Wain Stones stand in complete contrast to the gently rolling moors. A walk along the crest of Cold Moor leads back into Bilsdale.

Leave the car park at Chop Gate and follow the road up through the little village, passing the Buck Inn. Follow the Stokesley road up and downhill, then turn right as signposted for St Hilda's Church. The road bends left at a higher level, near **Bilsdale Hall**, so turn right through a gate as indicated by a public bridleway signpost. A track drops a little in a wood, then climbs up from the wood. The track forks on an open slope, so keep left and keep climbing. Pass a shale spoil heap on a slope of bracken, then keep climbing to pass a low stone building, where a few blasted pines grow on the bracken slope. Go through a small gate in a stout stone wall and note the entrenchment beyond, where an **earthwork** has been cut around the head of the dale.

Climb further up a slope of bracken using a clear and obvious path. Join and follow a broad and clear track that runs straight ahead, rising gently across heathery **Urra Moor**. After passing a few shooting butts, you will later reach a junction of tracks. The idea is to turn left here,

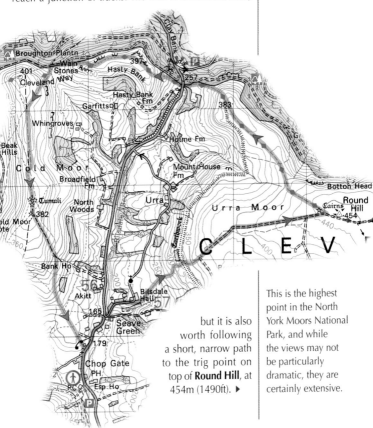

but it is also worth following a short, narrow path to the trig point on top of **Round Hill**, at 454m (1490ft). ▶

This is the highest point in the North York Moors National Park, and while the views may not be particularly dramatic, they are certainly extensive.

Urra Moor rises beyond the forested gap of Clay Bank

The trig point on Round Hill sits on the squat remains of a moorland burial mound. The North York Moors are dotted with similar mounds, and some parts are criss-crossed by ancient earthworks that were either territorial markers or defensive structures. The moorland marker known as the **Hand Stone** probably dates from the 18th century. It has two open palms inscribed with the near-indecipherable words: 'this is the way to Stoxla' (Stokesley) and 'this is the way to Kirbie' (Kirkbymoorside). The older Face Stone features a crudely carved face.

After turning left along the moorland track, follow the course of the Cleveland Way around the head of Bilsdale. A gritty or stone-paved path descends on a wide heather moorland slope. After crossing a broad dip, you will eventually reach the Carr Ridge. Go through a gate and follow a stone-paved path steeply downhill. Go through another gate to reach the B1257 on **Clay Bank**. ◄

Summer weekend Moorsbus services use this road.

Cross the road and climb some 60 stone steps as signposted for the Cleveland Way. Continue up a steep, stone-paved path on a bracken slope. This suddenly levels out as a stone-paved path along the moorland crest of

Hasty Bank, around 390m (1280ft). Enjoy views stretching across the plains, as well as around Bilsdale. Keep to the right of the blocky outcrops of the **Wain Stones** to find a steep and rugged path, requiring some hands-on scrambling down to a grassy gap. Climb from the gap and go through a gate, then turn left to leave the Cleveland Way and take a path climbing diagonally uphill.

Turn left along a moorland crest and follow a narrow but clear path past a cairn at around 390m (1280ft) on **Cold Moor**. Keep going across a slight dip on the heathery crest and continue along a clear track. Pass the heather humps of **tumuli** on Three Howes and fork left along a rugged path to start descending a moorland slope. This path approaches a forest, then follows a wall down to a gate. Go through the gate to find a rugged, enclosed track that can be muddy. Go through gates on the way down between fields; at first the track becomes easy and grassy, although later it narrows and can be muddy. It suddenly reaches a Methodist chapel, and a short cobbled road leads down to a tarmac road. Turn left then almost immediately right to follow the B1257 down through **Chop Gate**. Walk past the Buck Inn on the way back to the car park and toilets.

The jagged gritstone outcrops of the Wain Stones seen on Hasty Bank

WALK 18

Kildale, Ingleby Moor and Battersby Moor

Start/finish	Kildale Railway Station, NZ 604 095
Distance	16.5km (10¼ miles) from Kildale, or 10.5km (6½ miles) from Warren Moor
Total ascent/descent	410m (1345ft)
Time	5hrs 15mins or 3hrs 15mins
Terrain	A fairly easy walk along minor roads and moorland tracks, with one less-trodden path, but the high moors are exposed in bad weather
Maps	OS Landranger 94; OS Explorer OL26 North
Refreshments	Glebe Cottage Tearoom at Kildale
Transport	Northern trains serve Kildale from Whitby and Middlesbrough

Kildale is a tiny village with good access to the Cleveland Hills. This route follows a road from Kildale on to Warren Moor, then takes a path down to Baysdale Abbey. Good tracks are used to climb on to Ingleby Moor, then the route follows the Cleveland Way over Battersby Moor to return to Warren Moor. The walk is structured from the railway station at Kildale, but you can drive up the road to Warren Moor and park, which shortens the walk by 6km (3¾ miles). Alternatively, this walk can be combined with Walk 19, also starting from Kildale, to offer a much longer day's exploration.

Motorists could park beside this high road, which will be followed again later in the day.

Leave Kildale Station, where there are toilets, and walk up the road, passing Glebe Cottage Tearoom. Turn right to leave the little village and turn left along another road at a junction, heading straight towards the steep slopes of Park Nab. The road heads off to the right and climbs uphill, swinging right until it crosses a cattle grid on a high corner of the road on **Warren Moor**, at 335m (1099ft). ◄

A public bridleway signpost points left to indicate a narrow path across the heather moor. Walk downhill, roughly parallel to a line of old fenceposts and a drystone

106

wall. Go through a small gate and look down through a rough pasture to spot another small gate. Go through it and walk further downhill, turning right to reach a narrow tarmac road. Turn left down the road and cross a bridge to approach the big house of **Baysdale Abbey**, which has several other buildings alongside. The house stands on the site of a 12th-century Cistercian nunnery, of which little remains.

Turn right before reaching the house and go through a gate bearing a waymark arrow to enter a large field. Veer slightly left across the field to spot a gate at a point where a wall and fence meet. Go through the gate and climb through the next field to reach another gate giving access to a forest. Turn right along a track after entering the forest. The track winds uphill and becomes a lovely grassy carpet, leaving the forest at another gate.

Continue along and up the grassy track on a moorland crest of heather and bilberry, with the surface underfoot becoming stony while passing the stump of an old stone cross set in a socket. Further uphill, on the right, is a gritstone outcrop. The track rises further and eventually levels out on **Ingleby Moor**. Avoid a track heading off to the right, but wait until the track you are following runs slightly downhill, then take the

Baysdale Abbey stands on the site of a 12th-century nunnery

next clear stony track to the right. This track passes shooting butts, bends to the left as it climbs, then runs straight up the heathery slope with boundary stones alongside. It reaches the ancient tumulus of **Burton Howe** at 424m (1391ft) and joins another clear track.

Turn right to follow the track downhill alongside **Greenhow Bank**. This is part of the Cleveland Way, which is followed all the way back to Kildale, but first keep an eye out for the Guide Stone away to the right.

GUIDE STONE

From 1711 it was a requirement that signposts and guidestones were erected on remote moorland routes, and the stone markers outlived the wooden ones. The 18th-century Guide Stone is easily missed in poor visibility, lying well away from the track. It offers the following misspelled directions: 'Ingleby and Stoxley' (Stokesley), 'Kirby and Hemsley' (Kirkbymoorside and Helmsley) and 'Gisbro' (Guisborough). Of interest to cash-strapped walkers is a hollow on top of the stone that usually contains a few coins left for needy wayfarers.

Keep walking northwards along the track until another track, signposted for the Cleveland Way, branches off to the right at a gate. This track leads along another moorland crest over **Battersby Moor**, eventually reaching a gate at a road bend. Follow the road straight ahead. (Motorists who parked here earlier in the day finish at this point.) The road crosses a rise on **Warren Moor**, turns left over a cattle grid at a corner, then runs down around the slopes of Park Nab to reach a broad and green valley. When you reach a road junction, turn right for **Kildale**. To return to the railway station, turn left as signposted.

The Guide Stone is a moorland marker where cash is left for needy travellers!

WALK 19

Kildale, Leven Vale, Baysdale and Hograh Moor

Start/finish	Kildale Railway Station, NZ 604 095
Distance	15.5km (9½ miles)
Total ascent/descent	430m (1410ft)
Time	5hrs
Terrain	A moderate walk along clear tracks and paths, although some parts are more rugged; minor roads are used at the start and finish
Maps	OS Landranger 94; OS Explorer OL26 North
Refreshments	Glebe Cottage Tearoom at Kildale
Transport	Northern trains run to Kildale from Whitby and Middlesbrough

Just one obscure road leads to the farming settlement at the head of Baysdale, and another road crosses the barren moorland slopes in the middle of the dale. Only those who are prepared to stride along the moorland flanks of the dale will discover the old tracks and paths that once carried all the traffic in and out of it. This route, starting and finishing in Kildale, also includes little Leven Vale, where the remains of an old ironstone mine can be seen. At another point the route is only a short walk from the little village of Westerdale, although this is barely in view.

Leave Kildale Station, where there are toilets, and walk up the road, passing Glebe Cottage Tearoom. Turn left as signposted for Commondale. Walk alongside the boundary wall encircling Kildale Hall, then turn right as signposted for **Little Kildale**. Pass the few cottages that make up this tiny settlement and follow the road up a forested slope. It becomes a broad dirt road as it climbs from the forest into fields. Turn right as signposted along a public bridleway just before reaching **Warren Farm**. Walk down through a field, noting a **chimney** that is the only remaining part of the former Warren Moor Ironstone Mine in Leven Vale.

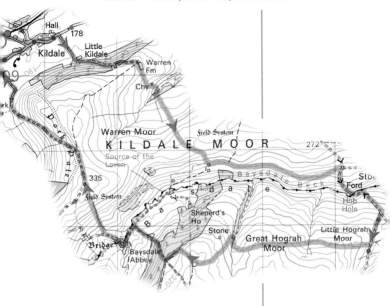

Cross a beck and go through two gates to walk up alongside a large field. Go through a small gate and continue up the heather and bilberry slopes beyond. The path is rough and stony and goes through a gate on the crest of **Kildale Moor**. Follow it down the heather moorland slope towards three buildings, and turn left as signposted along a bridleway from the first of the buildings. A grassy track, stony in places, runs easily across the bracken and heather slopes of **Baysdale**. It eventually rises to a lonely moorland road junction. Turn right downhill to reach a ford and footbridge at **Hob Hole**. Follow the road uphill and turn right at a junction where there is a 'no through road' sign. Walk up the road to look over into Westerdale.

Leave the road by turning right as signposted along a public bridleway and follow a rutted track up the heather slopes of **Little Hograh Moor**. This soon becomes a rutted path across the slope, marked with cairns, and crosses a small beck. Later, **Great Hograh Moor** becomes quite

A chimney at the Warren Moor Mine in Leven Vale

111

bouldery and the path passes a memorial cairn. Walk down to cross a neat little arched stone bridge next to a gnarled oak tree at Great Hograh Beck. Climb straight uphill and turn left up a clear track. Follow this up a heather moorland slope and when it levels out, turn right along a very narrow path marked by a small cairn. Cross the heather moor and descend to a junction of drystone walls. Turn left to walk beside a forest until a clear track is reached. Turn right to follow it through a gate and down through the forest, emerging at a house.

Go down the access track away from the house and turn left to walk alongside Baysdale Beck. Turn right to walk through a farmyard and pass close to the big house of **Baysdale Abbey**. ◄ Follow the tarmac access road across a bridge and head uphill a short way. Turn right at a bridleway signpost, then turn left to walk uphill and go through a small gate. Look up a slope of rough pasture to spot another small gate, then walk uphill and go through it. You will reach heather moorland and a narrow path that runs parallel to a wall and a line of old fence posts. It reaches 335m (1099ft) on **Warren Moor**, where there is a road and a cattle grid.

Turn right to cross the cattle grid, then walk down around the slopes of Park Nab to reach a broad and green valley. When you reach a road junction, turn right for **Kildale**. To return to the railway station, turn left as signposted.

The house stands on the site of a 12th-century Cistercian nunnery, of which little remains.

Walkers forge their way across the heather slopes of Little Hograh Moor

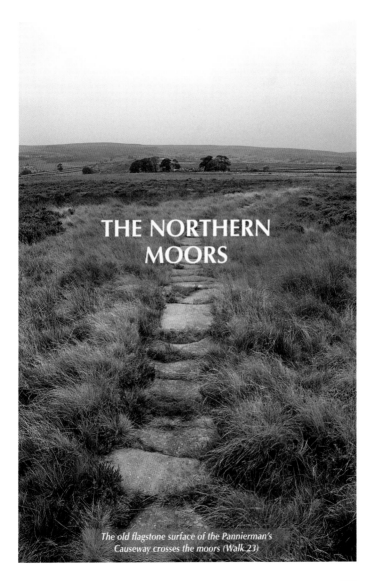

THE NORTHERN MOORS

The old flagstone surface of the Pannierman's
Causeway crosses the moors (Walk 23)

THE NORTHERN MOORS

The Northern Moors rear up from the plains with great gusto, Roseberry Topping – the Yorkshire Matterhorn – in particular, raising rugged flanks to a fine peak. There are other steep slopes nearby, such as those rising to Easby Moor and Captain Cook's Monument, or the forested slopes rising from Guisborough, but on the whole the Northern Moors lack distinctive features, and present a vista of gently rolling uplands of no great height, petering out eastwards as cultivated fields and wooded valleys lead to the coast.

Wild moorland walking is quite limited in this area. Walkers who have followed the course of the Cleveland Way will recall the prominent monument on Easby Moor, and the arduous detour to Roseberry Topping. They will also recall the fiddly nature of the route through Guisborough Woods, and the way the route seems to forsake the high ground altogether, leaving the National Park and heading across country to reach the coast at Saltburn. It takes a bit more effort to discover the Northern Moors, as well as careful route-finding where paths are not particularly well trodden. The area used to be criss-crossed with prominent tracks, but the moorland has almost engulfed them, leaving only rugged grooves, marooned marker stones and occasional lengths of stone-flagged causeways.

Four walking routes are described in this area. The first is a popular circuit from Great Ayton, taking in Easby Moor and Roseberry Topping. Next is a walk from Guisborough, wandering through Gisborough Woods. A route from Danby takes in the empty moorlands around Siss Cross, but also links some of the villages along the flanks of Eskdale. A final route runs from Scalby Dam to Danby, offering the chance to visit the Moors National Park Centre before heading back over Danby Beacon. Paths can be quite vague, but the discovery of travellers' ancient trails is one of the delights of walking over these moors.

Public transport around the Northern Moors is remarkably good, and the area can be approached on a daily basis throughout the year using Arriva buses and Northern trains that run from early until late. Additional summer weekend Moorsbus services run to and from the Moors National Park Centre near Danby, where visitors will find plenty of useful information.

WALK 20

Great Ayton, Easby Moor and Roseberry Topping

Start/finish	High Green, Great Ayton, NZ 563 107
Distance	10.5km (6½ miles)
Total ascent/descent	430m (1410ft)
Time	3hrs 30mins
Terrain	A short walk, but tough in places, along clear roads, tracks and paths, with some steep slopes
Maps	OS Landranger 93; OS Explorer OL26 North
Refreshments	Pubs, restaurants and cafés at Great Ayton
Transport	Northern trains serve Great Ayton from Middlesbrough and Whitby. Summer Sunday Moorsbus services link Great Ayton with Guisborough and Helmsley

Walkers regularly visit Captain Cook's Monument on Easby Moor and climb the 'Yorkshire Matterhorn' of Roseberry Topping. This route starts in the village of Great Ayton, where James Cook was educated, then climbs on to Ayton Moor. After taking in the monument, the route follows the course of the Cleveland Way, staying high all the way to Roseberry Topping. After enjoying views from the summit, walkers can descend to Aireyholme Farm, where James Cook lived as a youth, and ponder whether he ever climbed Roseberry Topping! Various paths link to return through the fields to Great Ayton.

Start on the High Green in the village of Great Ayton. There are plenty of places offering refreshments, as well as shops, a post office, toilets and a tourist information centre, tel 01684 722835. Follow Station Road and later cross the bridge over the line at **Great Ayton Station**, then turn right along a short access road signposted as a public footpath. Go through a gate at the end of the track and cross a beck. Go through a gate or kissing gate and turn left along a tarmac track. When you reach a junction, turn right and follow a narrow road. This gives way to a

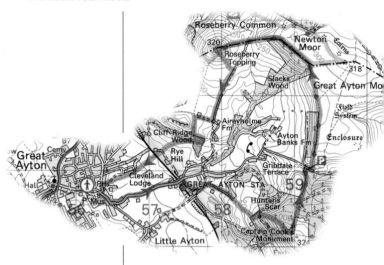

path that gradually steepens as it climbs, offering views of Roseberry Topping and the Cleveland Hills rising from the plains.

As the gradient eases, watch out for a marker post on the left. Turn left and follow a path up to a forest. Climb straight up a clear, worn path, cross a grassy track and continue straight up through the forest. A grassy path leads out on to the heather top of Easby Moor, and you will naturally be drawn straight to the prominent stone obelisk of **Captain Cook's Monument**, standing at 324m (1063ft).

A fine stone obelisk, **Captain Cook's monument** is 15m (51ft) high and overlooks Marton, the suburb of Middlesbrough where James Cook was born in 1728, and Great Ayton, where he received an education from 1736 to 1740. Cook's father was employed at Aireyholme Farm, the owner of which, Mr Scottowe, paid for James' education at the Michael Postgate School, now the Captain Cook Schoolroom Museum. The inscription on the obelisk states, 'In memory of Captain Cook the celebrated navigator. A man in nautical knowledge inferior to none. In zeal, prudence and energy superior to most. Regardless of the danger, he opened an intercourse with the Friendly Isles and other parts of the Southern Hemisphere. Born at Marton in 1728. Massacred at Owyhee (Hawaii) 1779.'

Turn left to follow a stone-paved path away from the monument, pass a memorial to a crashed aircraft, and walk down a track on a forested slope. Turn right along a minor road, then almost immediately turn left up a flight of 115 steps. The gradient eases on **Great Ayton Moor**, where there is a wall and a clear-felled forest to the left and heather moorland to the right. Simply follow a clear track onwards, at around 290m (950ft), keeping the wall always on the left. The wall suddenly turns a corner on **Newton Moor** where there is a gate and a signpost for Roseberry Topping. Zigzag steeply down a stone-paved path, levelling out on a grassy gap. Another stone-paved path winds steeply up the rugged slopes of **Roseberry Topping** to reach bare sandstone slabs and a trig point at 320m (1050ft).

Quarried and scarred, and undermined for ironstone, leading to partial collapse in 1907, **Roseberry Topping** has suffered greatly through the years, but has by no means been diminished. The 'Yorkshire Matterhorn' bears its scars proudly and presents an

The unmistakeable profile of Roseberry Topping

aggressive face to the plains. Enjoy the views from this airy perch, looking out across the plains to the distant Pennines and industrial Teesmouth, as well as round the Cleveland Hills and North York Moors, even taking in a small stretch of the Cleveland coast.

Retrace steps back across slabs of rock, but fork right down another stone-paved path to descend a steep slope of bracken. Go through a small gate and walk down a grassy slope to pass through a large gate at the bottom. Turn right down a clear track, going through a gate to approach **Aireyholme Farm**. Walk through a gate and almost into the farmyard, but turn right through another gate signposted as a public footpath. Follow a track up alongside a field to a little cottage, and turn left alongside a fence as marked. ◄

The rugged little hill nearby, where 'whinstone' was quarried until 1973, is now the Cliff Rigg Quarry Nature Reserve.

Follow the fence to a corner and turn left to cross a step-stile, then go through a nearby kissing gate to walk down a path on a wooded slope. Continue straight through a junction of paths to enter a field, then swing right. From that point always walk straight ahead through the fields, crossing an access road, then crossing a railway line with care. Again, take care when the path eventually emerges on an awkward bend on Newton Road. Turn left to walk back to the finish point at the High Green in **Great Ayton**.

The prominent little peak of Roseberry Topping is seen here at sunset

WALK 21

Guisborough, Gisborough Moor and Hutton Village

Start/finish	Market Cross, Guisborough, NZ 615160
Distance	13.5km (8½ miles)
Total ascent/descent	310m (1015ft)
Time	4hrs 15mins
Terrain	A moderate walk along good forest and moorland paths and tracks; the route takes in a low-level railway trackbed towards the end
Maps	OS Landrangers 93 and 94; OS Explorer OL26 North
Refreshments	Plenty of pubs, restaurants and cafés around Guisborough
Transport	Regular Arriva buses serve Guisborough from various places, including Whitby, Stokesley and Middlesbrough

Guisborough is a bustling little town with a broad main street flanked by cobbled areas. Its most outstanding feature is a ruined priory set in a quiet green space near the town centre. Extensive woods and forest fill the slope between the town and Gisborough Moor, and the Cleveland Way traverses this slope, taking in the viewpoint of Highcliff Nab. Clear tracks cross the open moors beyond the forest, passing close to the remote farm of Sleddale. The route from Hutton Village back to Guisborough follows the course of a disused railway line through the suburbs.

Start at the Market Cross in Guisborough, and maybe take the time to visit the priory ruins, or save a visit until later. Follow Bow Street, which is the way the traffic goes to Whitby, but when most vehicles turn left, keep straight on along Belmangate. Pass beneath an old railway arch and at the top end of the road is Gracelands Care Home, where a public footpath sign points further uphill. The path is flanked by trees and bushes as it climbs between fields to reach the lower edge of **Guisborough Woods**.

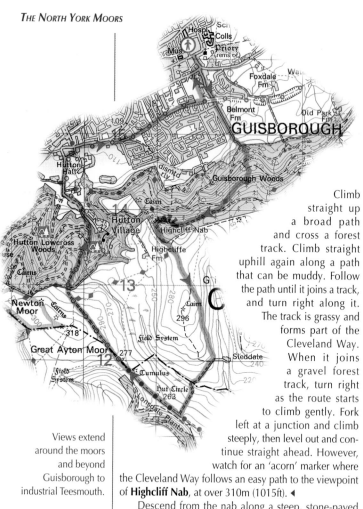

Climb straight up a broad path and cross a forest track. Climb straight uphill again along a path that can be muddy. Follow the path until it joins a track, and turn right along it. The track is grassy and forms part of the Cleveland Way. When it joins a gravel forest track, turn right as the route starts to climb gently. Fork left at a junction and climb steeply, then level out and continue straight ahead. However, watch for an 'acorn' marker where the Cleveland Way follows an easy path to the viewpoint of **Highcliff Nab**, at over 310m (1015ft). ◀

Views extend around the moors and beyond Guisborough to industrial Teesmouth.

Descend from the nab along a steep, stone-paved path, turning left towards a stand of stout beech trees beside a field near **Highcliffe Farm**. Go through a gate where the Cleveland Way turns right, but follow a track straight ahead across the moors. The track crosses the slopes of Codhill Heights, then joins an access road

leading away from the remote farm of **Sleddale**. Turn right to follow it, crossing a little valley on the way up to a road junction on Percy Cross Rigg.

Turn right and walk up the road at a gentle gradient, passing an enclosure containing five **Iron Age hut circles**. The tarmac road ends at a gate on **Great Ayton Moor**, and a sandy track rises beyond, signposted as a public bridleway, becoming rough and stony as it gains height. Pass a wartime pillbox at the top, at around 300m (985ft), then head downhill. Note the course of the Cleveland Way to the right before reaching a forest gate.

Go through the gate and follow the track straight downhill through **Hutton Lowcross Woods**, avoiding all other tracks on the slope to land on a road just outside **Hutton Village**. Follow Hutton Village Road through a sort of grassy parkland where fine individual trees spread their boughs. Watch out for the access roads for **Hutton Hall** and The White House, both of which are private, but just alongside is a short access road signposted as a public footpath. Follow this as it narrows to become a path leading to a junction with the busy Hutton Lane.

A fine viewpoint is reached at Highcliff Nab

A cyclist on the old moorland track between Percy Cross Rigg and Hutton Village

Follow the lane a little way towards town to find nearby bus stops, as well as access to an old wooded railway trackbed running parallel to the road. Follow the trackbed away from an old station platform and later walk along a bit of Aldenham Road to pick up another stretch of the old line alongside a row of houses. The line runs through a green space between modern housing estates, then crosses a road. Keep straight ahead and follow the trackbed on a wooded embankment. It eventually crosses a bridge over Belmangate, but turn left beforehand and go down the steps. Follow a path past Guisborough Rugby Club and Guisborough Cricket Club, then follow Bow Street straight into the centre of **Guisborough**.

GISBOROUGH PRIORY

Founded in 1119 by Robert de Brus, Gisborough Priory was a powerful Augustinian house. The priory church was rebuilt around 1200, but was destroyed in 1289 by a fire caused by a plumber working on the roof. Many artefacts were also lost in the blaze. After it was rebuilt, the priory was again wrecked by raiding Scots, but eventually it assumed its full stature, which visitors can still appreciate to some extent by marvelling at the towering arch of the east window. Entry is free, but a donation is appreciated, tel 01287 633801.

WALK 22

Danby, Siss Cross, Commondale and Castleton

Start/finish	Danby Railway Station, NZ 707 084
Distance	14km (8¾ miles)
Total ascent/descent	280m (920ft)
Time	4hrs 30mins
Terrain	A moderate moorland walk where the initial moorland path needs careful route-finding, but other paths and tracks are clear; the route ends with a low-level valley walk
Maps	OS Landranger 94; OS Explorer OL26 North
Refreshments	Duke of Wellington Inn and Stonehouse Bakery Café at Danby; Cleveland Inn at Commondale; Eskdale Inn off-route at Castleton
Transport	Summer weekend Moorsbus services to Danby from Pickering and Guisborough; Northern trains from Whitby and Middlesbrough link Commondale, Castleton and Danby

The little village of Danby in Eskdale is a natural starting point for walks, having regular rail services and summer weekend Moorsbuses. This day's walk climbs on to Danby Low Moor and visits Siss Cross before heading down to Commondale. A low-level walk along tracks leads from Commondale towards Castleton and so back through Eskdale to Danby. Of course the walk could be finished early, or altered in terms of start and finish, by catching a train between any of the three railway stations: Danby, Commondale and Castleton. With more time to spare, walkers could head for Danby Lodge and the Moors National Park Centre, although a visit there is included in Walk 23.

Leave the railway station and walk straight up the road through the village of Danby, passing the Duke of Wellington Inn. There is also a shop and café/bakery nearby. The road, which heads uphill, is signposted for

The stone upright of Siss Cross offers views around the bleak moorlands

Scaling and Whitby and crosses a cattle grid. Just before reaching 'slow' painted on the road, turn right up a clear path to short-cut a road bend. Cross the road at **Rosedale Intake**, where a sign that reads 'Danby' is mounted on a roadside stone. A public footpath signpost points on to an open moorland. Be sure not to follow the broad grassy path ahead, but keep a little to the right along a narrower trodden path. This path forges up the gentle heather slopes of **Danby Low Moor** and crosses a path known as the Pannierman's Causeway. The way uphill is occasionally marked with yellow blobs of paint or small cairns. Note that the trodden path drifts away from the right of way marked on the map, heading for an upright stone that can be seen on the skyline. This is **Siss Cross**, standing at 268m (879ft). From here sweeping views can be enjoyed across Eskdale to the High Moors.

Pass Siss Cross and drift a little to the right along a vaguely trodden path, to link with a wheel-marked groove through the heather. This reaches a clear, stony track on the heather moor at a public bridleway signpost on **Gerrick Moor**. Turn left to follow the track, which is plain and obvious. Note the green hump of Freebrough Hill away to the right, rising above farmland. The track has been worn into a deep, muddy puddle where it crosses a dip in the moorland. This may be impossible to pass dry-shod, and the moorland on either side is also soft and wet. The track beyond is pleasant and easy, eventually reaching a road junction beside the appropriately whitewashed **White Cross**, at 264m (866ft).

Walk straight ahead along and down the road signposted for Commondale, which is much quieter than the other road on the moorland slope. Before the road rises on **Sand Hill**, watch for a public bridleway signpost on the left. Pick up stretches of a flagged causeway across a slope of bracken, then later turn left and go down through three small gates to reach the little village of **Commondale**. ▶ The Cleveland Inn offers food and drink, and there are also toilets.

Turn left along a minor road as signposted for the station. Fork left at **Fowl Green Farm**, and the tiny railway station can be found down to the right if required.

> Notice the preponderance of brick buildings, rather than stone, as the village was essentially founded on a brickworks.

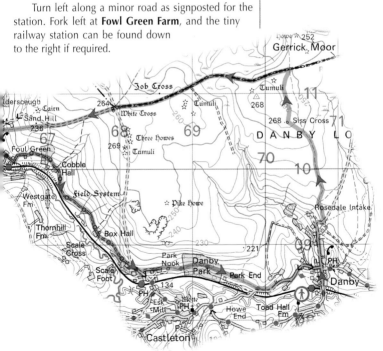

However, to continue with the route, stay on the track and climb for a while to enjoy good views over Eskdale. The track runs through oak and birch woods, where permitted paths allow further exploration. Drop down to a few houses at **Cobble Hall**, then follow the track across a moorland slope above, and roughly parallel to, the railway line. The track passes **Box Hall** and rises to cross a cattle grid at Firbank, where you will reach a minor road. Turn right downhill, passing a sign for Castleton mounted on a roadside stone. You could follow this road all the way down to the railway station or the Eskdale Inn, but the route doesn't go that far, turning instead left along a farm access track signposted as a bridleway.

Pass farm buildings at **Park Nook**, and go through a couple of gates to follow a grassy track gently down to a gate leading into woods at **Danby Park**. The woodland is mostly birch, and a clear path runs across the slope to exit at another gate. Follow a grassy path straight onwards across a bracken slope, and continue straight ahead along and down a minor road. There are two public footpath signposts on the right later: one in a dip and one over the next rise on the road. Either of them could be used to return directly to the railway station at **Danby**, otherwise continue along the road to reach the Duke of Wellington Inn in the village.

The walk passes fine woodlands near Commondale

WALK 23

Scaling Dam, Clitherbeck, Danby and Beacon Hill

Start/finish	Scaling Dam Sailing Club, NZ 740 125
Distance	13.5km (8½ miles)
Total ascent/descent	240m (790ft)
Time	4hrs 30mins
Terrain	A moderate moorland walk where vague or untrodden paths at the start and finish need care; other moorland paths, tracks and roads are clear
Maps	OS Landranger 94; OS Explorer OL27 North
Refreshments	Duke of Wellington Inn and Stonehouse Bakery Café at Danby; café at the Moors National Park Centre
Transport	Regular Arriva buses pass Scaling Dam; summer weekend Moorsbus services to Danby from Pickering and Guisborough; Northern trains serve Danby from Whitby and Middlesbrough

Traffic hurtles along the busy A171 at Scaling Dam, and there is also a good bus service along the road. From here you can discover some remarkably bleak moorlands using all-but-forgotten paths and tracks. One such path is the Pannierman's Causeway, which is virtually lost in its early stages, but gradually reveals its course and ultimately becomes a fine flagstone causeway. Lord's Turnpike is a good track leading down to Danby, offering a chance to visit the Moors National Park Centre. Danby Beacon makes a fine viewpoint, taking in the Northern Moors and High Moors, before a track across the moors and a rather vague path lead back to Scaling Dam.

There is a car park at Scaling Dam Sailing Club, safely off the busy A171. Apart from the sailing club premises there are toilets and bird hides, and the western end of the reservoir is a nature reserve to which there is limited access. Start the walk by leaving the car park and turning left to walk along busy Moor Road. Walk on the right-hand side, on the grass verge, facing oncoming

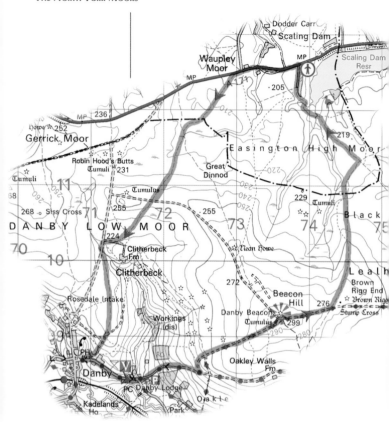

traffic for safety. Continue to the road junction signposted for Grinkle and walk just a short distance beyond it on **Waupley Moor**.

There is a public bridleway signpost and a small gate on the left-hand side of the main road. Go through the gate and swing to the right among some gorse bushes to find a vaguely trodden path. This leads to a gravel strip across a boggy patch, then the trodden route requires care is taken to follow it correctly. Pass a nearby tree

and aim southwest towards a vague dip in the skyline ahead, pushing through a large area of bracken to reach heather moorland beyond. Look carefully for a groove in the heather, which leads to a prominent upright boundary stone with two smaller stones crouched beside it. However, step to the right to reach a smaller upright stone nearby.

A boundary stone is a landmark during the first moorland ascent

Follow a vaguely trodden path onwards through the heather to approach a large rushy area in a dip at Water Dittins, and be sure to spot a wooden post that marks the position of a low footbridge. ▶ Once across, follow a narrow trodden path that weaves gradually uphill through a series of parallel grooves on a heather moorland slope. Pass a few gorse bushes and a lonesome pine tree, and note a marker stone where old grooved pathways intersect. The placename of 'Whitby' is written as 'BY WHIT' on one face, and a mangled version of 'Castleton' can be discerned on another face.

Feet are usually wet before reaching the footbridge!

Step across a minor road as signposted public bridleway, at almost 250m (820ft), then continue down a groove in the heather moorland. Later, watch carefully to join and follow a flagged causeway. This is the Pannierman's Causeway, and it is good to see at least some stretches of it running clearly across the moor. Step across an access track near **Clitherbeck Farm** and aim for a road crossing a stream nearby. Once the road has crossed the stream, turn left along a clear track signposted as a public bridleway. This is obvious underfoot all the way across a heather moor. When you reach a drystone wall, swing right at a complex junction of tracks and be sure to take the track that drops the most steeply downhill on the left. Go through a gate, near some houses, where you will reach a battered road that quickly leads on to another road. Either turn right down Briar Hill to go into the village of **Danby**, or left along Lodge Lane to reach the Moors National Park Centre at **Danby Lodge**, where this route heads.

> **Danby Lodge** used to be a shooting lodge but now serves as a visitor centre for the North York Moors National Park. Displays and exhibits focus on conservation, to encourage sensitive and thoughtful recreation. Maps and guides are on sale, and there is a café and toilets on site. The countryside nearby is open for exploration and summer weekend Moorsbus services run to and from the centre to encourage visitors to leave their cars behind. To check opening times, tel 01439 772737.

Leave the centre and take the road signposted for Danby Beacon, following it uphill through fields and over a cattle grid. Turn left at a road junction and the road bends right before running straight up to the highest part of the heather moorland. The summit of **Danby Beacon** is cluttered with a signpost, tumulus, beacon post, view indicator and a trig point at 299m (981ft). Views around the northern half of the North York Moors are particularly extensive.

Walk gently down along a broad and stony track signposted for Lealholm. Turn left as signposted along a public bridleway, and immediately fork right along a grassy path that soon narrows on heathery **Lealholm Moor**. Although narrow, the path has a few cairns along its length and is clear enough to follow easily across Black Dike Moor. You will reach an area of short-cropped grass next to a little valley where there are a few trees on **Easington High Moor**. Continue along the track, but watch out on the left for a marker post.

A rather vague, narrow path crosses the heather moorland. Aim for a tall wooden post to stay on course. Once you reach the post, you will get a glimpse of Scaling Dam in the distance. Head towards the reservoir and a fence will lead down to the left to reveal a gate and footbridge. Cross the footbridge and walk along a duckboard path between fences. Head uphill to the left, then turn right and go through a gate. A grassy track heads straight towards busy Moor Road, but before reaching it, turn right along a footpath that leads through a small wood to return directly to the car park beside **Scaling Dam**.

Danby Beacon, high point of the walk at 299m (981ft).

THE HIGH MOORS

A fine view of upper Bilsdale can be enjoyed on the descent from the moors (Walk 25)

THE HIGH MOORS

For many walkers the High Moors are the best part of the North York Moors National Park – extensive rolling moorlands are cleft by a dozen verdant dales, the plateau-like nature of the uplands being determined by the sandstone cap that protects lower, softer and more crumbly limestones and shales from weathering. The sandstone generates a rather acidic soil that favours moorland vegetation, and some wetter parts develop peat bogs. The limestones and shales exposed in the deeper dales allow grasslands suitable for pasture to flourish, and some of the level areas may even be tilled.

The High Moors are criss-crossed with paths and tracks. Many of the paths are based on ancient cross-country trading routes linking one dalehead with another, while other routes avoid the dales altogether and soar across broad moorland 'riggs' to get through the region as quickly as possible. Many of the ancient routes were waymarked by stone 'crosses'. In some cases these were actually carved as crosses, while in others they were simply squared stumps of rock inscribed with various placenames, and many of the old inscriptions are now barely decipherable. They were often carved by barely literate hands and contain wildly inaccurate and variable spellings! Later tracks were installed to allow vehicle access for grouse shooting and general moorland management.

A dozen fine walks explore the High Moors, and many of the routes lie close to each other or have a path in common, so there is scope to switch from one to another, varying and extending the routes. Two walks start from Chop Gate at the head of Bilsdale, exploring the moors on either side of the dale, and two more wander high above Farndale. Two walks explore Spaunton Moor, one from Hutton-le-Hole and the other from Rosedale; and two are based on the old Rosedale Railway, one making a circuit around the dale and the other running from Blakey to Battersby – from the moors to the plains. One walk explores Westerdale, while another three start from villages in Eskdale and climb high above Danby Dale, Great Fryup Dale and Glaisdale. Nor is that all, since the course of the Lyke Wake Walk is covered towards the end of this guidebook. It stays as high as possible on the High Moors, enjoying some of the places already visited, but also including additional tracts of broad, bleak and barren moorlands.

In the summer months when the heather is in bloom and the High Moors are flushed purple, they are a joy to explore, but in foul weather, poor visibility or when winter weather whips across them, they are best left to those who are good navigators. Even though many of the paths and tracks are clear and well trodden, a wrong turning can lead well off-course and cause a lot of inconvenience late in the day.

WALK 24

Chop Gate, Cock Howe, Ryedale and Wetherhouse Moor

Start/finish	Chop Gate car park, Bilsdale, SE 558 993
Distance	20km (12½ miles), or 14.5km (9 miles) using the Moorsbus service back from Fangdale Beck
Total ascent/descent	580m (1900ft)
Time	6hrs 30mins or 4hrs 30mins
Terrain	A tough walk, mostly along clear moorland paths and tracks, but some stretches are virtually untrodden; the high moors are exposed, but low-level field paths link the farms later in the walk
Maps	OS Landranger 100; OS Explorer OL26 South
Refreshments	Buck Inn at Chop Gate
Transport	Summer weekend Moorsbus services pass Chop Gate and Fangdale Beck, linking with Helmsley, Stokesley and Guisborough

This walk starts at Chop Gate (pronounced Chop 'Yat') at the head of Bilsdale and crosses from Bilsdale to Ryedale, then back to Bilsdale, exploring two parts of the broad and bleak expanse of Bilsdale West Moor. The immensely tall Bilsdale transmitter acts like a pivot for the walk, remaining a prominent feature in views throughout the day. After descending to the little village of Fangdale Beck, the route wanders from farm to farm along the valley sides back to Chop Gate. This low-level stretch could be omitted if you land on the road in time to catch the summer weekend Moorsbus service back to Chop Gate.

Leave the back of the car park at Chop Gate and cross a wooden bridge over **Raisdale Beck**. Follow a track up from a gate as marked, but watch for a footpath sign pointing up to the left. Climb straight uphill through a deep groove, but later leave it and continue up through fields and through a gate. Avoid a step-stile to the left, but

A tall mast forms a pivot around which the route makes a circuit

climb to a higher step-stile and cross it. Go up a steep, crumbling, slippery shale path on a bracken slope. The path passes to the left of a stand of pines and levels out on a heather moor. Although fairly clear, the path can be rugged in places and is marked with paint blobs. There is a cairn and an upright stone on **Cock Howe**, at around 400m (1310ft).

Continue straight onwards, crossing a track, to follow a narrow but obvious path down a heather moor. This leads to a beck that is crossed beside a large, split, half-dead and half-living rowan tree. Climb uphill and keep to the right-hand side of a wall on a grassy moorland. Go through two metal gates beside a plantation of pines where you will reach the access track leading away from **Head House**. Turn right to follow the track gently uphill across the moorland slopes of Arnsgill Ridge, after which the route becomes a gradual descent. Go through a gate and down a track through fields towards **Rye Farm**.

Turn left just before reaching a farmhouse, to walk down a steep, rugged grassy slope and forge through a wet rushy patch to find a footbridge over Arns Gill. Climb up to a small gate in a wall and go through it, then turn right up a deep-cut groove full of heather and bilberry. A stony and grassy track continues alongside a wall, then leads down the moorland slope, through a gate and on to a minor road near **Plane Tree Farm**.

Turn left to follow the road beside a wood, then later the road wriggles down to **Lane House**, where a public bridleway signpost points left through a gate. Walk down through a field and through another gate, then down through the next field and swing left through a gap. Walk down to a gate and ford **Blow Gill** in a wooded valley. Follow a narrow path up a bracken slope, away from the river on to a heather moor. Keep following the only narrow path uphill, taking care not to lose sight of it. The path turns right and left as it climbs, and both turns are indicated by marker posts. Trees come into view and there is a glimpse of a remote farmstead at **Low Thwaites**.

Turn left to follow a clear track alongside a wall, heading gradually uphill. Turn right around a corner of the wall, then look for a narrow path heading off to the left, linking a line of upright stones and concrete posts planted across **Wetherhouse Moor**. The path and posts lead into a shallow valley on the moorland, where you will cross a little beck in a wet and boggy area. Continue along the narrow path, in a heathery groove, to pass a cairn on the moorland slope. Follow the path faithfully, as it is the only real trodden route downhill. One wet stretch has been surfaced with gravel.

Take care when following it more steeply down a deep groove on a bracken slope, as the ground underfoot is uneven. Go through a couple of small gates, down a field, through a gate and turn right. Turn left out of a garden at The Forge and walk along a tarmac road through the little village of **Fangdale Beck**. Either walk to a telephone kiosk at a road junction and turn left along the B1257, or cross a footbridge over the River Seph, climb the steps and turn left along the road. ◄

If a summer weekend Moorsbus is due, then the final 5.5km (3½ miles) to Chop Gate can be omitted.

Follow the road only until a farm access road on the left is signposted as a public footpath. Cross a bridge over

the River Seph to reach **Low Mill** and note the old mill and its race. Pass between the buildings and turn right as marked, then go through a gate as marked, walking gently up alongside a field. Go through a gate and keep right alongside another field. Go through another

137

gate and turn right along an access road. Branch left between the farm buildings at **Stable Holme** and keep left up a short, overgrown track.

Go through a gate and simply walk straight across a slope, following a path that can be overgrown with bracken. Walk up the access road to **Beacon Guest** and cross a stile to continue along an overgrown path. To keep on course, bear in mind that you should always have a drystone wall on your right. The path is muddy later, then climbs across a field. Turn right through a gate, head downhill and swing left to find a track leading through gates towards **Crookleith Farms**. Avoid the farms by walking straight down through a field as marked from a gate, and turn right to find a footbridge over a little beck. Cross and turn left, then quickly right, using tracks signposted as a bridleway. Turn right again as signposted at a house and walk alongside a field. Turn left and walk uphill alongside a field, and keep going straight over a rise to reach **Orterley Farms**.

Turn right in the farmyard, go through a gate, then turn left and cross a ladder stile. Proceed as marked through fields, but bear in mind that it can be very wet and muddy down beside the river. If that proves to be the case, then traverse a little further up the slope. Eventually turn right and cross a wooden bridge to return to the car park and toilets at **Chop Gate**. If food and drink are required, then head a short way up the road to the Buck Inn.

A view encompassing the moorlands, woodlands and fields of upper Ryedale

WALK 25

Chop Gate, Tripsdale, Bransdale and Bilsdale

Start/finish	Chop Gate car park, Bilsdale, SE 558 993
Distance	17.5km (11 miles), or 13km (8 miles) using the Moorsbus
Total ascent/descent	500m (1640ft)
Time	5hrs 30mins or 4hrs
Terrain	A tough walk, mostly along clear moorland paths and tracks, but some stretches are virtually untrodden; the high moors are exposed, but low-level field paths link the farms later in the walk
Maps	OS Landranger 100; OS Explorer OL26 South
Refreshments	Buck Inn at Chop Gate
Transport	Summer weekend Moorsbus services pass Chop Gate and Fangdale Beck, linking with Helmsley, Stokesley and Guisborough

Starting from Chop Gate at the head of Bilsdale, this walk crosses the hidden, wooded Tripsdale, traverses the empty moors above Bransdale, then heads back to Bilsdale. It explores the broad and bleak expanse of Bilsdale East Moor, and while most paths and tracks are clear, some short stretches are rather vague. After descending to Bilsdale, the route wanders from farm to farm along the valley sides before returning to Chop Gate. This low-level stretch could be omitted if you reach the road near Fangdale Beck in time to catch the summer weekend Moorsbus service.

Leave the car park at Chop Gate and turn right to walk along the B1257. There is a public footpath signpost on the left, close to the access road for Esp House. Walk diagonally up through a field, then turn left up the access road for **William Beck Farm**. Turn right in front of the house, then right again along a short grassy track to a gate. Turn left up a sunken, walled, grassy track to reach another gate. Walk straight up a field and go through yet another gate, then follow a narrow path up a bracken slope and continue

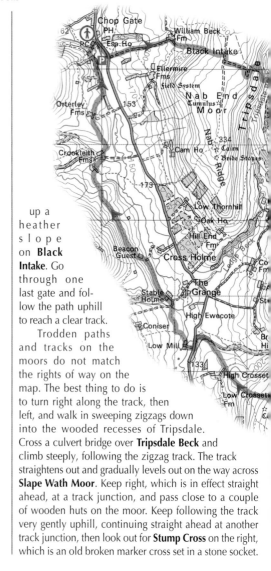

up a heather slope on **Black Intake**. Go through one last gate and follow the path uphill to reach a clear track.

Trodden paths and tracks on the moors do not match the rights of way on the map. The best thing to do is to turn right along the track, then left, and walk in sweeping zigzags down into the wooded recesses of Tripsdale. Cross a culvert bridge over **Tripsdale Beck** and climb steeply, following the zigzag track. The track straightens out and gradually levels out on the way across **Slape Wath Moor**. Keep right, which is in effect straight ahead, at a track junction, and pass close to a couple of wooden huts on the moor. Keep following the track very gently uphill, continuing straight ahead at another track junction, then look out for **Stump Cross** on the right, which is an old broken marker cross set in a stone socket.

The track runs almost to 420m (1380ft) along Bransdale Ridge, with good views down into the lovely Bransdale. Follow the track gently downhill on the heather moorland to reach a barrier gate and minor road. Only a few paces along the road a public footpath sign points right across a moorland with the curious name of **Botany Bay**. Follow a very narrow trodden path through the heather, passing a boundary stone. ▶ Follow the path down to the corner of a drystone wall, then keep right of the wall and follow it down to a little beck called Bonfield Gill. Masses of squelchy rushes provide a firmer footing when crossing the stream.

This bears the letters K and H.

Walk uphill alongside another drystone wall to reach a stand of pines at a corner of the wall. Climb straight uphill along a rather vague path and cross a clear track. Forge ever upwards at a gentle gradient on the moor, but watch for the line of the path by spotting a series of small cairns. Eventually, you will gain views over the broad heathery crest into Bilsdale. If the correct line is followed to Black Holes, the vague path crosses a clear track and descends to go through a gate in a drystone wall.

Walkers cross Tripsdale before climbing on to the moors

If a summer weekend Moorsbus is due, then the final 5.5km (3½ miles) to Chop Gate can be omitted.

Walk down through two fields and go through a couple of gates that are fairly close together. Aim as if for the head of Bilsdale, walking down a grassy slope beside a fence. Go through a couple more gates and continue walking alongside a fence. Another gate leads into a wood where the path runs down through a very deep-cut groove. It can be wet and muddy towards the bottom, where a gate gives way to the **B1257**. ◄

Turn left along the road, but only as far as the access road to Low Mill, on the right, which is signposted as a public footpath. Cross a bridge over the River Seph to reach **Low Mill**, noting the old mill and its race. Pass between the buildings and turn right as marked, then go through a gate as marked, walking gently up alongside a field. Go through a gate and keep right alongside another field. Go through another gate and turn right along an access road. Branch left between the farm buildings at **Stable Holme** and keep left up a short, overgrown track.

Go through a gate and simply walk straight across a slope, following a path that can be overgrown with bracken. Walk up the access road to **Beacon Guest** and cross a stile to continue along an overgrown path. To keep on course, bear in mind that you should always have a drystone wall on your right. The path is muddy later, then climbs across a field. Turn right through a gate, head downhill and swing left to find a track leading through gates towards **Crookleith Farms**. Avoid the farms by walking straight down through a field as marked from a gate, and turn right to find a footbridge over a little beck. Cross and turn left, then quickly right, using tracks signposted as a bridleway. Turn right again as signposted at a house and walk alongside a field. Turn left and walk uphill alongside a field, and keep going straight over a rise to reach **Orterley Farms**.

Turn right in the farmyard, go through a gate, then turn left and cross a ladder stile. Proceed as marked through fields, but bear in mind that it can be very wet and muddy down beside the river. If that proves to be the case, then traverse a little further up the slope. Eventually turn right at a wooden bridge to return to the car park and toilets at **Chop Gate**. If food and drink are required, then head a short way up the road to the Buck Inn.

The route passes the broken shaft of Stump Cross high on heathery Bransdale Moor

WALK 26

Low Mill, Harland, Rudland Rigg and West Gill

Start/finish	Low Mill, Farndale, SE 672 952
Distance	13km (8 miles)
Total ascent/descent	360m (1180ft)
Time	4hrs 30mins
Terrain	A moderate but long walk starting on field paths, followed by a climb up on to a moorland slope and across rough pasture; firm, clear stony tracks lead across the high moors, and a rugged path is used for the descent; the high moors are exposed
Maps	OS Landrangers 94 or 100; OS Explorer OL26 South
Refreshments	None on the route. The Feversham Arms and Daffy Caffy lie off-route at Church Houses
Transport	None

Rudland Rigg is a long and sprawling moorland to the west of Farndale. A rough stony road runs along its crest, and this could be followed all the way through the North York Moors from Gillamoor to Kildale, taking walkers over some of the highest moors with relative ease. Walkers traversing Rudland Rigg will notice dozens of curious humps and bumps; these are the remains of bell pits where poor-quality coal was dug from the bedrock. On this walk it takes time to reach Rudland Rigg, but walkers will find that the rest of the day unfolds rapidly along good tracks across the high moors.

Start at Low Mill, where there are toilets in a car park. Walk down the road and cross a bridge, then climb straight up the road as signposted for Gillamoor. The road eventually bends left, at which point leave it as signposted along a public footpath through the garden of a house. Walk straight up a field to a higher house and cross a tarmac road. Walk up through another field to reach a gate leading into a wood, where there are good views around Farndale. Go through a gate at the top of

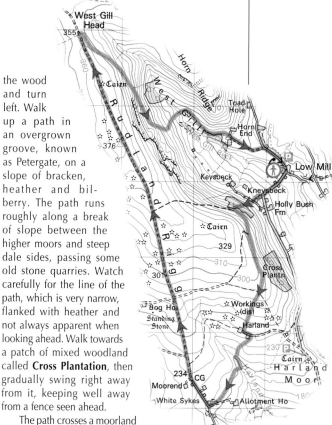

the wood and turn left. Walk up a path in an overgrown groove, known as Petergate, on a slope of bracken, heather and bilberry. The path runs roughly along a break of slope between the higher moors and steep dale sides, passing some old stone quarries. Watch carefully for the line of the path, which is very narrow, flanked with heather and not always apparent when looking ahead. Walk towards a patch of mixed woodland called **Cross Plantation**, then gradually swing right away from it, keeping well away from a fence seen ahead.

The path crosses a moorland track to reach the corner of a drystone wall. ▶ A farm can be seen ahead in a gentle valley, so walk down towards it, alongside the wall, crossing a ladder stile and going down through fields. Keep to the left of the farm buildings at **Harland**, turning left along the access track to reach a neighbouring farm. Turn right and go through a gate between the farmhouse and a corrugated barn. Walk down through a

There is usually no objection to walkers turning right to follow the track straight towards Rudland Rigg.

field and go through another gate as marked. Keep going through fields, swinging left to walk parallel to Harland Beck. Watch carefully on the right to spot a footbridge. Cross over it and follow a clear, grassy path out of a tumbled, drystone-walled enclosure and go through another gate. Follow a heathery path, which can be squelchy in places, then use a wooded path to avoid **Allotment House**, reaching a small gate and a minor road.

A multitude of humps and bumps are the remains of old bell pits, where poor-quality coal was wrested from the ground.

Turn right to follow the road gently uphill, passing a building that was formerly a chapel. The road crosses a cattle grid to reach open moorland. When the road turns left and heads towards Bransdale, keep straight ahead and walk gradually uphill along a stony track flanked by heather moorland. There are a couple of patches of tarmac, as well as places where the track is worn down to bedrock that looks curiously like stone paving. ◄

Towards the top of the track it is possible to branch left to reach a trig point on **Rudland Rigg**, at an altitude of 376m (1234ft). There are good views around the High Moors, and the old road can be seen snaking onwards along the moorland crest. Follow the gently sloping track downhill, crossing a slight dip at **West Gill Head** where there are paths leading off to either side at 355m (1165ft). Turn right along a clear path at this point to begin the descent.

The path is rather rutted and leads down past a series of bilberry-covered shooting butts. Watch out for a cairn and swing right to follow the path to a solitary rowan tree on the bracken, heather and bilberry moorland slope. There are a couple of marker posts, then the path descends steeply and becomes more rugged for a while on a slope of bracken, becoming a fine grassy ribbon later. Go down through a gate in a wall, then turn left downhill as marked. Go through another gate in another wall and walk down to **West Gill Beck** to cross a footbridge. Turn right through a gate and go through another gate to follow a clear grassy track past the derelict High Barn. Keep to the track, through more gates, to pass **Horn End** and leave by following its access track downhill. When you reach a minor road, simply turn right to walk back into the little village of **Low Mill**.

FARNDALE DAFFODILS

Walkers who visit Farndale in spring should consider walking the easy riverside path between Low Mill and Church Houses, which links Walk 26 and Walk 27. The Farndale Nature Reserve, normally green and grassy, turns into a mass of yellow when the wild daffodils are in bloom. Visitors have made their way to Farndale for decades to enjoy this spectacle, and in the past many would pick a bunch, or even scythe them for collection and ultimate sale! Since 1955 the daffodils have been protected, and they are jealously guarded today – anyone caught picking them can be fined £5!

A flowery garden bursts into colour at the Old Post Office at Low Mill in Farndale

WALK 27

*Church Houses, Bloworth Crossing
and Farndale Moor*

Start/finish	Church Houses, Farndale, SE 669 975
Distance	19.5km (12 miles)
Total ascent/descent	320m (1050ft)
Time	6hrs
Terrain	A moderate but long moorland walk; minor roads give way to clear, firm, easy tracks across the moors; the high moors are exposed
Maps	OS Landranger 94; OS Explorer OL26 South and North
Refreshments	Feversham Arms at Church Houses; the Daffy Caffy is off-route at High Mill; the Lion Inn is off-route at Blakey
Transport	None, but summer weekend Moorsbus services pass the Lion Inn at Blakey, running to and from Danby and Pickering

Farndale is quite charming, while the moors that flank it are extensive, bleak and barren. However, the High Moors are also served by a loose network of tracks that allows walkers to eat up the distance while striding out along firm, dry and gently graded surfaces. Apart from the initial steep climb, this walk is actually quite easy, and route-finding is relatively simple too, but bear in mind that the moors are exposed in bad weather and shelter is very limited. This walk makes a fine circuit high around the head of Farndale from the tiny village of Church Houses, although walkers could also easily start and finish using the Moorsbus service to and from the Lion Inn on summer weekends.

Start at Church Houses near the head of Farndale, where the Feversham Arms offers food, drink and accommodation. Set off along a road signposted 'Farndale (West Side)', walking downhill to cross a bridge, then climbing steeply to a road junction. Turn right, as signposted for Dale End, to reach **Monket House**. Turn left as signposted for Bransdale from a gate. Follow a broken concrete road uphill through another gate, then climb past a couple of bare humps of shale. Keep following a gravel track up a slope of heather, bracken and bilberry, and keep straight ahead at junctions with other tracks. At a higher level there is more heather cover and the track levels out. After reaching a track intersection at **Ouse Gill Head**, at 369m (1211ft), turn right.

Simply follow a broad clear track that climbs gently uphill and across the high moors, at just over 400m (1310ft). Of particular interest along the way are a series of old marker stones bearing curious placename spellings. Look out first for a stone on the right marking the 'Kirby Rode'. Keep to the track, passing intersections with footpaths and bridleways, and note broken Cockam Cross well off to the left, marking 'Stoxli Rode' and 'Brans Dale'. Later, the chunky **Cammon Stone** is on the right. The track rolls along across the moors, and the aim is to keep walking straight ahead and avoid a couple of tracks leading off to the left. Pass a leaning stone that declares the way to 'Kirby Moor Sid', then a few more paces lead up to an intersection of tracks at **Bloworth Crossing**, at 388m (1273ft). The Cleveland Way runs to the left and straight ahead, but turn right to continue the walk around the head of Farndale.

The route passes the chunky Cammon Stone on the way to Bloworth Crossing

See Walk 30 and Walk 31 for historical notes about the old line.

Pass a barrier gate to walk along the trackbed of the former Rosedale Railway. ◄ First walk along a low embankment, then pass through a shallow cutting as the track curves left. Cross a moorland beck on a little embankment and then the cutting at **Middle Head**, which can be a bit wet and muddy. The track curves and crosses another little embankment across another moorland beck, and provides fine views over Farndale from **Dale Head**. Gentle curves give way to a long low embankment that slips over the moorland crest, so that you look down into Westerdale for a change. When you reach a junction with tracks that lead down into Farndale and over to Westerdale, keep straight ahead.

The old railway trackbed rises very gently and overlooks Farndale again from **Farndale Moor**. On the way uphill there are more curves, then suddenly, as you reach a shallow cutting, the **Lion Inn** can be seen on a moorland crest across a valley. The trackbed makes a great curve around the valley and the inn passes from sight, but it can be reached by making a short detour along a path rising to the left. Staying on the trackbed, however, you will soon reach a gate and a road junction on Blakey Ridge. ◄

Summer weekend Moorsbus services can be caught here, or at the Lion Inn.

The return to Farndale is simple and straightforward. Turn right and follow the road steeply downhill, as signposted for Farndale, and the moorland slopes give way to rough pastures and green fields. Simply keep walking straight ahead at junctions to return to **Church Houses** and the Feversham Arms.

The Lion Inn can be reached by a short detour from the route

WALK 28

Hutton-le-Hole, Ana Cross, Spaunton Moor and Lastingham

Start/finish	Ryedale Folk Museum, Hutton-le-Hole, SE 705 900
Distance	12.5km (7¾ miles)
Total ascent/descent	250m (820ft)
Time	4hrs
Terrain	A moderate moorland walk where paths need care at first, being vague in places; the route follows good tracks later, and paths towards the end are good too; the high moors are exposed
Maps	OS Landranger 94 or 100; OS Explorer OL26 South
Refreshments	Pub and tearooms at Hutton-le-Hole; pubs at Lastingham
Transport	Summer weekend Moorsbus services to Hutton-le-Hole from Pickering and Danby, as well as Monday-only Ryecat buses from Pickering

Hutton-le-Hole is a charming village that spans a stream and sits where the Tabular Hills give way to the high heather expanses in the heart of the North York Moors. Take care over route-finding on the initial ascent, as paths are rather vague and it is all too easy to be drawn off along clearer tracks. The top of Spaunton Moor is crowned with Ana Cross, and from that point a clear track descends directly towards Lastingham. The village can be explored, or walkers can simply head straight back along a low-level series of paths to return to Hutton-le-Hole and the splendid Ryedale Folk Museum.

Leave Hutton-le-Hole by taking the road signposted for Lastingham, passing a car park and toilets on the edge of the village. A little further up the road, turn left along a grassy track and go through a gate. Follow an obvious, gentle, grassy path up a heather moorland slope. Turn left later along narrow Lodge Road, and follow it until you reach a post bearing marker arrows at **Wheat Lund**. ◄ Turn right to leave the road and follow another clear, grassy

The road continues to Spaunton Lodge.

track up the broad heather moorland crest of **Hutton Ridge**. The path joins this clearer track and turns right at around 250m (820ft).

Follow the track gently down the heather moor to cross a beck. The track rises and falls towards another beck, but turn left before reaching it, following a path to ford the beck near a stone sheepfold where the ground is wet and boggy. Continue up through a firm grassy area on the heather moor and keep following the path to reach a road at a public footpath signpost. ▸

If you miss the path altogether and follow the track to the road instead, simply turn left up the road to continue.

Turn left and walk up the road at a gentle gradient to reach Chimney Bank at 312m (1024ft), then turn right along a clear track from a barrier gate. There should be no mistaking the landmark of **Ana Cross** ahead, which is reached by branching right from the track. It stands on a tumulus on top of Spaunton Moor at over 290m (950ft).

Follow a clear and obvious track due south from Ana Cross. Keep right at a junction of tracks and keep walking straight downhill. In fact, simply keep to the broadest and clearest track on the moorland slope, passing **Spring Heads** until the stony surface finally gives way to a grassy one. There is a Millennium Stone beside a signposted junction of paths just before the track reaches a gate. The village of **Lastingham** can be explored by going down through the gate and returning to this point later. The route, however, turns right.

Ana Cross is a prominent moorland marker planted high on Spaunton Moor

The little village of **Lastingham** is huddled between the Tabular Hills and High Moors and can easily be explored by making a detour down from the route. Of particular interest is St Mary's Church, with its Norman crypt and Shrine of St Cedd, originally built in 1078 on the site of an ancient Celtic monastery. Food and drink are available from the Lastingham Grange Hotel and Blacksmith's Arms.

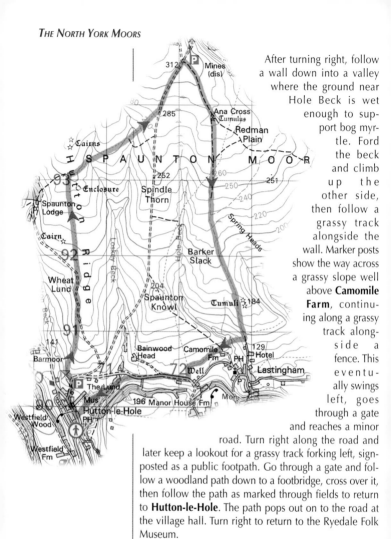

After turning right, follow a wall down into a valley where the ground near Hole Beck is wet enough to support bog myrtle. Ford the beck and climb up the other side, then follow a grassy track alongside the wall. Marker posts show the way across a grassy slope well above **Camomile Farm**, continuing along a grassy track alongside a fence. This eventually swings left, goes through a gate and reaches a minor road. Turn right along the road and later keep a lookout for a grassy track forking left, signposted as a public footpath. Go through a gate and follow a woodland path down to a footbridge, cross over it, then follow the path as marked through fields to return to **Hutton-le-Hole**. The path pops out on to the road at the village hall. Turn right to return to the Ryedale Folk Museum.

Hutton-le-Hole has a long history of settlement dating back to Neolithic times. The village was mentioned in the Domesday Book as 'Hoton', but throughout the ages it has also been rendered as 'Hege-Hoton', 'Hoton under Heg' and 'Hewton'. As a placename Hutton-le-Hole dates only from the 19th century. The village features the Ryedale Folk Museum, Crown Inn, tearooms, accommodation and gift shops.

RYEDALE FOLK MUSEUM

Trace the history of Yorkshire folk from 4000BC to 1953, with plenty of hands-on exhibits, as you wander from one part of the museum site to another. Over a dozen buildings have been erected since 1964, some with roofs supported by enormous cruck frames (pairs of curved wooden timbers supporting the ends of the roof), some standing in isolation, while others are arranged as a row of small shops. Vintage vehicles, including motorised and horse-drawn carriages, are preserved, and land around the site sprouts vegetables and flowers, including many varieties of cornfield flowers. Local folk often give demonstrations of traditional crafts while wearing period dress. There is an entrance charge, and the museum incorporates a shop and toilets, tel 01751 417367 www.ryedalefolkmuseum.co.uk.

A view of Hutton-le-Hole and the moorland slopes of Spaunton Moor beyond

WALK 29

Rosedale Abbey, Hartoft,
Lastingham and Ana Cross

Start/finish	Rosedale Abbey, SE 724 959
Distance	14km (8¾ miles)
Total ascent/descent	350m (1150ft)
Time	4hrs 30mins
Terrain	A moderate moorland walk where farm roads give way to rugged paths that can be muddy in places; moorland paths and tracks become firmer later, and the high moors are exposed
Maps	OS Landranger 94 or 100; OS Explorer OL26 South and OL27 South
Refreshments	Pubs and tearooms around Rosedale Abbey; pubs at Lastingham
Transport	Summer weekend Moorsbus services to Rosedale Abbey from Pickering and Danby, as well as Monday-only Ryecat buses from Pickering

Rosedale is a charming pastoral dale, but explorers don't need to climb too far up the valley sides to discover wild and rugged slopes. This route wanders along the valley side from the neat stone village of Rosedale Abbey to pass Hartoft on a rugged moorland slope. Staying on the moorland fringe, the route passes close enough to Lastingham for a quick visit to be possible, then climbs over the top of Spaunton Moor to reach Ana Cross. A rapid descent leads back to Rosedale Abbey via the steep slopes of Rosedale Chimney Bank.

Leave the village green at Rosedale Abbey and follow the road signposted for Pickering. Turn right before the Coach House Inn to follow a narrow road signposted for Thorgill. A sign warns motorists of 1:3 (33%) gradients on Rosedale Chimney Bank, but walkers don't climb that far. Turn left at the White Horse Farm Inn, along

A path on the edge of the moor above Lastingham.

a clear track passing a couple of farmhouses. The track eventually ends at **Hollins Farm**, but just before reaching the farm turn right, as signposted along a bridleway, up a grassy track. Follow the path beside the drystone wall, not the path climbing straight up the moorland slope.

The path leads through bracken, at first fairly close to the wall, then drifts further away and further uphill from the wall. It contours across a slope of dense bracken and heather, passing below curiously named Cumratph Crag. ▶ Eventually the path rises from bracken slopes to heather moorland above **Hartoft**, although the moor is cut with great swathes of bilberry and crowberry too. Descend to the corner of a drystone wall and continue straight ahead beside it. There are a few trees around here, and a farm access road is joined near **High Askew**. Follow the road uphill away from the farm.

After reaching the top of the road, just before a cattle grid, turn right to follow a path beside a wall, on the edge of the heather moor. Follow the wall downhill, and ford Tranmire Beck. Climb uphill and continue along a grassy track with a wall, woodland and fields to the left and open moorland to the right. After crossing a rise, follow the track down to a signposted intersection of paths and tracks beside a Millennium Stone near **Lastingham**. The village is close enough to be easily visited and explored. ▶

Watch out for a cast-iron plaque marking the point where in Elizabethan times there was a glass furnace, for which Rosedale was once famous.

See Walk 28 for facilities and points of interest.

Turn right to follow a grassy track uphill, which soon becomes a broad and stony track on wide heather moorland. Follow the track past **Spring Heads** and keep climbing gently. Keep left at a junction of tracks and aim straight for the landmark **Ana Cross** on the horizon, standing on a tumulus on top of Spaunton Moor at over 290m (950ft). Walk past the cross and turn left along another broad and clear track. This leads to a barrier gate and a minor road at the top of Rosedale Chimney Bank, at 312m (1024ft).

Some walkers might be happy to turn right and follow the steep road straight downhill to return to Rosedale Abbey, but most of the road can be avoided as follows. Walk a short way down the road and turn left at a small car park. Follow a gravel path past some stone arches and continue above cottages at **Bank Top**. Turn right to walk just a short way down the access road, then keep left of three trees, well away from the cottages. Follow a vague grooved path, which becomes a clearer grassy groove bending left downhill. Continue down a narrow path on a steep slope of bracken, crossing stiles and turning right and left as marked on the little Red House Golf Course. Cross a narrow road and walk straight down through a field to reach a road beside a house. Cross a bridge and walk straight back into the village of **Rosedale Abbey**.

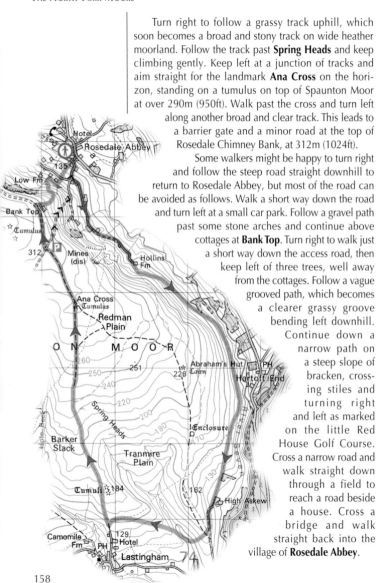

WALK 30

Rosedale Ironstone Railway around Rosedale Head

Start/finish	Rosedale Abbey, SE 724 959
Distance	17.5km (10½ miles)
Total ascent/descent	330m (1080ft)
Time	6hrs
Terrain	An easy but long walk, mostly on a firm and level moorland track, although field paths at the start and finish can be steep and muddy in places
Maps	OS Landranger 94; OS Explorer OL26 South and OL26 North
Refreshments	Pubs and tearooms at Rosedale Abbey; the Lion Inn is off-route at Blakey; the Dale Head Farm Tea Garden is also off-route
Transport	Summer weekend Moorsbus services to Rosedale Abbey from Pickering and Danby, as well as Monday-only Ryecat buses from Pickering. Summer weekend Moorsbus services link the Lion Inn with Pickering and Danby

The Rosedale Ironstone Railway ran from 1861 to 1926 so that large deposits of ironstone could be stripped from the high moors. Some initial processing of the ore was carried out in massive stone kilns, and trains pulled up to 15 loaded wagons at a time along the line around the head of Rosedale and away to Middlesbrough. The old trackbed running high around Rosedale can easily be made into a circular walk by using paths to climb up to it and descend from it, starting and finishing in the village of Rosedale Abbey. The old railway trackbed runs anywhere from 250m to 370m (820ft to 1215ft), but is so gently graded that in effect it contours around the dale.

Leave the village green at Rosedale Abbey and follow the road signposted for Pickering. Turn right before the Coach House Inn to follow a narrow road signposted for Thorgill. A sign warns motorists of 1:3 (33%) gradients on Rosedale

Chimney Bank. Walkers can use the road if they wish, but there is a different way uphill along paths. Follow the road across a bridge, then take a footpath straight uphill from a house, through a field, to cross another minor road. Walk up on to the little Red House Golf Course and turn right and left as marked over ladder stiles and left again up a steep slope of bracken. Follow a grassy groove up a heather moorland slope and swing right to pass three trees well to the right of cottages at **Bank Top**. Follow the access track uphill, away from the cottages, to link with the old railway trackbed. A short detour left along a gravel path leads to a set of eight stone arches where ironstone was roasted before being loaded on to railway wagons

The altitude of the trackbed at this point is around 300m (985ft). A chimney stood nearby until 1972, hence the name **Rosedale Chimney Bank**.

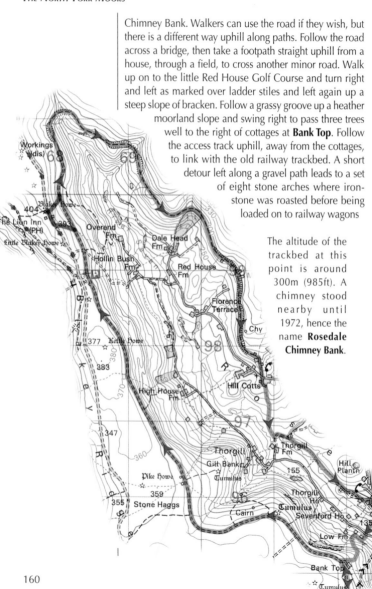

Double back and follow the old railway trackbed from a barrier gate, enjoying fine views over Rosedale. Pass a wooden bench and follow the stony or cinder track across a moorland slope of heather and bilberry. The trackbed makes a big loop around Thorgill Head, then passes a crumbling ruin at Sheriff's Pit. Keep going through a shallow cutting, although the trackbed is generally perched on a moorland edge overlooking Rosedale. Later, it is possible to reach a road on the left at Blakey Bank, at around 370m (1215ft), otherwise keep straight ahead. ▶ Cross a track and later there are two signposts pointing up to the left for the **Lion Inn** at Blakey, which is well-placed for a lunch break, especially on a wild day.

There used to be a few cottages nearby, housing railway workers.

LION INN AT BLAKEY

Blakey is a bleak spot, but food, drink and accommodation are offered at the celebrated Lion Inn, at over 400m (1315ft). The inn was once popular with the coal and ironstone miners who worked on the moors, and is popular today with walkers, bikers and motorists. Summer weekend Moorsbus services link the Lion Inn with Danby and Pickering, and the inn naturally offers an alternative start and finish point for this walk.

Keep following the cinder trackbed across heather moorland slopes, passing a brick wall with an arched window. The trackbed is on a raised embankment as it swings right to cross the headwaters of the River Seven at Rosedale Head. Some parts of the track are a bit muddy, and one boggy cutting is best avoided by using a path above it.

Cross another curved embankment at Reeking Gill, then follow an easier and firmer stretch of the old line. Another cutting is firm, dry and grassy, followed by another embankment at Nab Scar. Go round another curved embankment and follow a broad and grassy stretch of the old trackbed, but avoid spurs rising to the left. Pass a small ruin and four big crumbling stone buttresses. Next, pass below the stump of a **chimney** and admire 16 stone arches where ironstone was once roasted. Keep left of the last crumbling buildings, which are the remains of a

View across Rosedale from the old railway trackbed to the Lion Inn at Blakey

once-busy area known as The Depots, to go through a gate. Follow a track down to **Hill Cottages**.

Cross a minor road and continue down another track signposted as a public footpath. Go through a kissing gate and walk down beside a field, then go through another kissing gate and walk straight down through a couple of fields to follow a stone-paved path. Do not cross a footbridge near **Thorgill Farm**, but turn left to walk downstream beside the River Seven. Follow a track that can be muddy, but when it climbs away from the river, watch for a path marked off to the right. Look for more markers and gates to proceed downstream through fields and a wood before climbing away from the river to later follow an access road through a caravan site. ◀ Also watch out for a glimpse of a little church on the left, then turn left to follow a short path out of the site. Walk through a churchyard to return to the village green in the middle of **Rosedale Abbey**.

Bear in mind that facilities on the site are private.

ROSEDALE ABBEY

Only a small section of spiral stairway remains of the original 12th-century Cistercian nunnery, although the church occupies the same site. Facilities around the village include accommodation, pubs, tearooms, Abbey Stores, a car park and toilets. A glass workshop brings the process of glass-making back to Rosedale after an absence of several centuries!

*Rosedale Ironstone Railway
from Blakey to Battersby*

Start	Blakey Bank, Blakey Ridge, SE 683 989
Finish	Battersby Junction, NZ 588 072
Distance	16.5km (10¼ miles)
Total ascent	70m (230ft)
Total descent	310m (1015ft)
Time	5hrs
Terrain	Easy walking along a clear, firm trackbed across high moors and down through forest; the route follows minor roads at the end
Maps	OS Landrangers 93 and 94; OS Explorers OL26 South and OL26 North
Refreshments	The Lion Inn is close to the start on Blakey Ridge; the Dudley Arms is off-route at Ingleby Greenhow near the end
Transport	Summer weekend Moorsbus services link the Lion Inn with Pickering and Danby. Northern trains run from Battersby Junction to Middlesbrough, Danby and Whitby

After iron ore had been mined and roasted around Rosedale, trains carried up to 15 loaded wagons at a time away from the dale, around the head of Farndale. The wagons were divided into threes to be lowered down a 1:5 (20%) incline from the moors. The men who lived and worked on the moors at the top of the incline referred to their workplace as Siberia! The whole of the old railway line around Rosedale, as well as to Battersby Junction, is available for walkers, cyclists and horse-riders. As this is a linear route, walkers should use the summer weekend Moorsbus services to reach Blakey, then link with one of the Northern trains from Battersby Junction.

Start at a road junction on Blakey Bank, at around 370m (1215ft), which is also close to the junction of the old railway trackbeds. A blocked tunnel can be discerned under the road, where the railway passed from Rosedale to Farndale, and there is a parking space beside the road overlooking the old junction. The road signposted down to Farndale offers access to the old railway trackbed. Simply turn right along a track, signposted as a public bridleway, go through a gate and continue along the old line. There is no doubt about the way ahead, which is clear and obvious. A path heading off to the right later, incidentally, offers access to the celebrated **Lion Inn**. ◀

The walk can start at the Lion Inn by using this path.

The trackbed makes a great curve around a valley, then goes through a shallow cutting on **Farndale Moor**. The old line features a few curves as it descends gradually with good views into Farndale. However, as

The view down into Farndale from the old Rosedale Ironstone Railway

164

it follows a long low embankment, views into Farndale are obscured as the line slips across the moorland crest, and the head of Westerdale is seen instead. Views into Farndale are restored later, and the trackbed begins to curve again around **Dale Head**. A curved length of embankment crosses a moorland beck, then a cutting at **Middle Head** can be a bit wet and muddy. Cross another moorland beck on another curved embankment, then go through a shallow cutting. A low embankment leads to a barrier gate and a prominent intersection of tracks at **Bloworth Crossing**, at 388m (1273ft).

The Cleveland Way is signposted straight ahead and to the right. Follow the old trackbed straight ahead and pass another barrier gate. The Cleveland Way later heads off to the left, but our route remains on the old

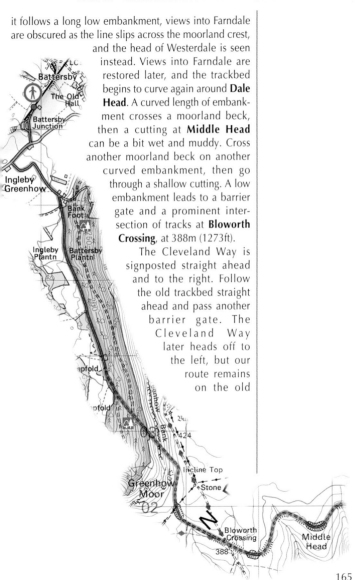

165

The 1:5 (25%) incline drops from Greenhow Bank to the plains

Wagons used to be unhitched from their engines at this point and lowered in relays to engines at the bottom of the slope, which has a gradient of 1:5 (20%).

line, passing through a little cutting at 410m (1345ft) on **Greenhow Moor**. Chunky blocks of masonry are all that remain of the old winding house at **Incline Top**. ◄ Simply walk straight down the old incline, which drops rapidly from the moorland, passing through a gate to enter a forest, then swing right at the bottom to continue on a level at 140m (460ft).

The last part of the old line cannot be followed, as it has been lost among fields.

A gate later leads out of the forest and the dirt road passes a few cottages, with views of the Cleveland Hills off to the left. However, the road is still well wooded and at times views are quite limited. **Battersby Plantation** stands to the right, almost all the way to a junction with a farm road at **Bank Foot**. ◄ Turn left and walk up the gentle incline of the road to reach a junction, then turn right as signposted for the station. Walk along the road and turn left for **Battersby Junction**, timing your arrival to suit one of the trains running towards Whitby or Middlesbrough. If too early for a train, detour first to Ingleby Greenhow, where the Dudley Arms offers food and drink.

WALK 32

Westerdale, Fat Betty, Westerdale Moor and Esklets

Start/finish	Parish church, Westerdale, NZ 664 058
Distance	14.5km (9 miles)
Total ascent/descent	360m (1180ft)
Time	5hrs
Terrain	A tough walk along farm tracks, field paths and moorland paths; the route follows a stretch of road on the high moors; the paths on the descent need care, being vague in places, as well as wet and muddy; the high moors are exposed
Maps	OS Landranger 94; OS Explorer OL26 North
Refreshments	None on the route, but available well off-route at Castleton and Blakey
Transport	None to Westerdale, but summer weekend Moorsbus services run over the higher moors to and from Danby and Pickering

The village of Westerdale, and indeed the dale itself, has the air of being well off the beaten track. Perhaps more walkers and cyclists visited it when Westerdale Hall Youth Hostel was in operation. There is no public transport into the dale, but anyone relying on public transport can easily restructure the walk to start high on the moors where Moorsbus services pass the Lion Inn and Ralph Cross. Starting from Westerdale, however, this walk climbs gradually to the High Moors, taking in sundry boundary stones and stone crosses, before descending into Esklets for a long stretch back through the dale, passing farms and cottages.

Leave the parish church in the lovely little village of Westerdale and follow the road uphill to reach a junction at a house called Pinfold. Turn left along a road, then either turn right at a gate, as signposted public footpath, or walk down to a crossroads and turn right along

Climbing from Westerdale to Castleton Rigg

Look up to Castleton Rigg to see the giant 'Seated Figure' sculpture on Castleton Rigg. The sculpture could remain in place until 2022.

Looking back across Westerdale from this point you can spot the prominent peak of Roseberry Topping.

another road, which the path quickly joins in any case. Either way, the road runs to **Broad Gate Farm**. ◄

Walk straight past the farm and continue through gates and alongside fields, then veer left, as signposted along a bridleway, to cross Tower Beck. Climb up a short wooded slope and walk up alongside a field to find a way to the farm at **Dale Head**. Pass between the buildings as directed and admire the fine old stonework. Go through a gate on to a moorland slope and follow a grooved path uphill. This becomes a grassy groove on a heathery slope, but the moorland magic is lost as it reaches a road junction on **Castleton Rigg**, at over 330m (1085ft). ◄

Turn right to walk up the road, passing **High Crag**, overlooking Botton. Note the boundary stones arranged in a sparse line to the right, each one with a white-washed top. Walk up the road, and as the road bends to the right, the boundary stones are suddenly arranged on the left. Follow a narrow moorland path from stone to stone through the heather, reaching the distinctive moorland marker of **White Cross**, also known as Fat

Betty, at over 410m (1345ft). ▸ Step across a nearby road, as signposted along a public bridleway, and veer to the right along a narrow path running gently down through the heather. Pass spoil heaps from old bell pits, as well as a boundary stone, then the path bottoms out and climbs gently, passing another boundary stone to reach a road at **Rosedale Head**. ▸

Cross the road and pass Margery Bradley Stone to follow a track away from the road. The track is clear and obvious, but keep right at a junction at **Flat Howe**, at over 420m (1380ft), and continue onwards until the path leads past some shooting butts. Watch carefully to switch to a vague path drifting more to the left, walking downhill alongside an extensive swathe of rushes. It is important to spot a stile over a fence. From that point drop more steeply down on to a grassier moorland shelf. Go through a gateway in a drystone wall and look for paint blobs and arrows leading off to the right down a rugged bouldery slope. Go through a gateway and walk down alongside a drystone wall, turning right at the bottom through another

Money may have been deposited on the stone for needy travellers.

The Lion Inn is about 1.5km (1 mile) away to the left.

'Fat Betty' or the White Cross is surely the most distinctive moorland marker

gateway. Cross a beck and follow a track up to another track at Esklets, and turn right to cross another beck.

Follow the clear track through a couple of gateways, when it becomes obvious that it is heading up to a stand of pines on a slope. Veer right as marked down

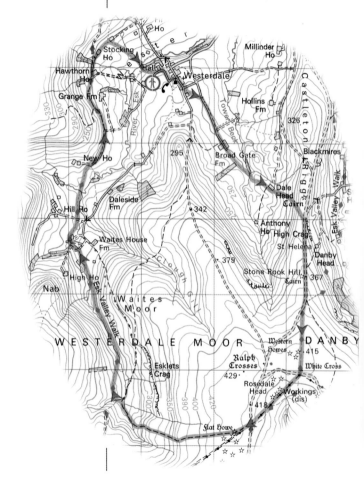

a narrow grassy path and go through a gate. Continue down through the valley, taking care to cross a small footbridge hidden among trees. Follow the path uphill from the bridge at first, then continue downstream, although some distance above the beck, on the rugged slopes of **Waites Moor**. Note the rowan trees and the mosaic of vegetation types on the slopes, but keep an eye on the narrow muddy path. Yellow paint blobs occur at intervals, then continue alongside a woodland before moving in among the trees as marked to reach a footbridge and farm access road below **High House**.

Cross the bridge and bear right, soon crossing another footbridge. Keep to the left of a farm, as marked at Wood End, crossing stiles and a farm access road below **Hill House**, followed by another footbridge while walking downstream through fields. Walk across a field and up through a field to reach a gate and farm access road near **New House**. Turn right to follow the road, with a drystone wall and fields down to the right and a bilberry moorland rising to the left. Continue this way until almost at **Grange Farm**, then as the track climbs towards mounds of shale spoil, veer right to go through a gate as marked. Look ahead for gateways while walking through fields, and keep to the left of the next farm buildings to follow another access road uphill from **Hawthorn House**.

Don't go too far up the farm access road, but branch right along a lesser track marked as a public footpath. Go in front of **Stocking House**, passing through gates, then once clear of the house go through a gate on the left. Continue walking ahead to reach Brown House and turn right into the garden. Walk straight downhill from the house, as signposted for Westerdale, through fields to cross a footbridge over the **River Esk**. Follow a track uphill, which can be muddy, then cross a pathless field to reach a gate and minor road. Turn left to follow the road past splendid Westerdale Hall, once a shooting lodge and youth hostel, but now a dwelling. The road leads back into the village of **Westerdale**, where a right turn leads back to the parish church.

WALK 33

Danby, Castleton, Botton Village and Danby Rigg

Start/finish	Danby Railway Station, NZ 707 084
Distance	14.5km (9 miles)
Total ascent/descent	450m (1475ft)
Time	5hrs
Terrain	A moderate walk along roads, tracks and paths through woods, fields and over high moors; some field paths require careful route-finding
Maps	OS Landranger 94; OS Explorer OL26 North
Refreshments	Duke of Wellington Inn and Stonehouse Bakery Café at Danby; Eskdale Inn, Downe Arms and Old Chapel Tearoom at Castleton; café at Botton; Fox and Hounds at Ainthorpe
Transport	Summer weekend Moorsbus services to Danby and Castleton from Pickering and Guisborough; Northern trains serve Danby and Castleton from Whitby and Middlesbrough

This walk essentially explores the low-lying reaches of Eskdale and Danby Dale, then climbs over the high moors of Danby Rigg. The first part of the walk is a simple stroll from Danby to Castleton in Eskdale. Towards the head of Danby Dale walkers have the opportunity to visit Botton Village, operated by the Camphill Trust, where agricultural and craft activities provide employment for over 300 people, many of them with special needs. After crossing Danby Rigg, the route returns to Danby, which is a natural transport hub in the dale with rail and Moorsbus services. The Moors Centre is within easy walking distance of the village if a visit is desired.

Leave the railway station and walk straight up the road through the village of Danby, passing the Duke of Wellington Inn. There is also a shop and café/bakery nearby. Turn left along the road signposted for Castleton, following it uphill, downhill and uphill again. When you reach a road junction, turn right, then immediately left along a grassy track, as signposted for Castleton and the Esk Valley Walk. This cuts across a bracken slope where it is necessary to keep left at a couple of path junctions. Go through a gate into a wood at **Danby Park**. The wood is mostly birch and a clear path runs across the slope to exit at another gate. Follow a grassy track through a couple of gates to pass farm buildings at **Park Nook**. Walk along the access road from the farm to a road, where a left turn downhill leads under the railway to pass the Eskdale Inn. Food, drink and accommodation are offered.

Cross a bridge over the River Esk and keep left to follow the road up into the village of **Castleton**. At the top of Station Road, to the right, lie toilets, the Downe Arms, Old Chapel Tearoom, post office and Co-op. However, turn left downhill, passing rows of stone houses, then turn right down Ashfield Road. Follow the road across Danby Beck to pass Ashfield Farm. Turn right after passing the access road for Brookfield Farm, along an overgrown public bridleway through bracken. Walk as directed, keeping well clear of the farmhouse, crossing a stone-slab bridge over **Danby Beck**. Go through several gates and fields, not always on a trodden path, looking ahead to spot all the large gates with blue waymark

Botton Village can be explored by making a short detour

A loop walk explores the village. Simply follow signposts for the Dairy, then walk straight downhill to return to the road junction.

arrows and/or Esk Valley Walk markers through **Danby Dale**. Eventually, you will reach a road junction.

Walk straight ahead at the junction, as signposted for Blakey, and follow the road up to West Green Farm and **Plum Tree Farm**. Walk straight along a grassy track, then go through gates to continue through fields, heading straight for **West Cliff Farm**. Follow the access track past another nearby farm, and keep straight ahead along a farm road to reach a road junction at **Stormy Hall**. Turn left down the road and pass a little chapel at the bottom. Keep left and follow the road uphill to another junction. A right turn at this point leads quickly to **Botton Village**, otherwise turn left. ◄

> **Botton Village** is operated by the Camphill Trust. There is a car park, shops, dairy and food centre. The community is essentially based around Christian family life, and over 300 people, many with special needs, live in family houses grouped in neighbourhoods around working farms. Agriculture and craft production are the main occupations. Everyone has a worthwhile, productive job and a place in the community. For information about the Camphill Trust, tel 01287 661294 www.cvt.org.uk/communities/botton-village.

Follow the road, then turn right up the East Cliff access road. Keep left of the farm as indicated, then turn right, then left to walk straight up through a field. Keep climbing and drift to the right in an enclosure full of bracken to reach a gate. Turn left through the gate, then swing right up a groove on a slope of bracken where the path can be squelchy. Drift left along a narrow path through heather on the higher slopes, passing a few small cairns on the way across **Danby Rigg**, touching 350m (1150ft). This rugged path, known as Jack Sledge Road, leads steeply down to a minor road in Little Fryup Dale. Keep left to walk down the road, but only to a junction. At that point turn left as signposted along a public bridleway and follow a green ribbon of a path that steepens along the rugged hillside until it becomes chiselled deep into the rock as it climbs on to the moorland brow. ▶

A short-cut path runs along the moorland brow, cutting out the descent into the dale and the need to climb back up. While not a right of way, it is well used.

Whichever route is chosen on the moorland brow, pass an upright stone marker and descend gently along the northern slopes of the moor, passing a larger upright stone. A gate takes the path off the heather moor and down between thick gorse bushes to land on a minor road near the Danby Tennis Club courts. Walk down the road and keep right, passing the Fox and Hounds at **Ainthorpe**, which offers food, drink and accommodation. At the bottom end of the village keep right as signposted for **Danby**, crossing a bridge over the River Esk to return to the railway station.

The walk passes an upright stone on the final descent from the moors

WALK 34

Lealholm, Heads, Glaisdale
Moor and Glaisdale Rigg

Start/finish	Lealholm Railway Station, Eskdale, NZ 762 078
Distance	22km (13¾ miles)
Total ascent/descent	500m (1640ft)
Time	7hrs
Terrain	A long and tough walk; minor roads give way to a farm track and vague hillside paths; a high moorland road gives way to clear moorland paths and tracks; the high moors are exposed, and the route finishes on minor roads
Maps	OS Landranger 94; OS Explorer OL27 North
Refreshments	Board Inn, Stepping Stones Cottage, Beck Hall and Shepherds Hall tearooms at Lealholm
Transport	Northern trains serve Lealholm from Whitby and Middlesbrough

Great Fryup Dale is one of many dales that link with Eskdale. A walk around it, taking in the moorland slopes on either side, is quite lengthy. This walk uses minor roads to cross the dale, then paths over a rugged hump to Fairy Cross Plain can be rather vague in places. After following a road on to the high moors, the route links with the course of the celebrated Coast to Coast Walk across the head of Great Fryup Dale, leading, in turn, on to the moorland crest of Glaisdale Rigg. The route then follows a moorland track and quiet country roads to return to Lealholm in Eskdale.

Leave Lealholm Railway Station by crossing the railway line and following a path straight down into the village, landing beside the Village Store and Beck Hall tearoom. Turn left, then right by road to cross an arched stone bridge over the River Esk and pass the Board Inn and Stepping Stones Cottage, which both offer food and drink. Follow the road straight uphill, passing a junction,

then turn right at a higher junction, passing a farm at **Wild Slack**, and right again downhill as signposted for Fryup. Keep walking down the road as signposted for Danby, then the road bottoms out and crosses a bridge over Great Fryup Beck. Climb straight up the road to pass **Furnace Farm** and follow the road as it bends left. Turn right up the access track for **Head House**.

A grassy track leads to Stonebeck Gate in Little Fryup Dale

Keep right of the farmyard and go through a gate into a field. Walk alongside the field with a wooded slope falling away to the right. Keep straight ahead along this line, through other gates and fields, to reach a moorland slope. The route, although untrodden at this point, is along a public bridleway that technically drifts left to reach the heathery crest of Heads at 270m (885ft). It then drifts right and is clear underfoot as it runs back downhill. ▶ Be sure to descend along a track well to the right of the pine-clad end of the crest. Go down through

If this line is overgrown, stay low and follow a boundary wall and fence onwards.

177

a gate and along a grassy track on a slope of bracken, passing a few pines. Keep left at a fork then later turn right through a gate, to follow a grassy track downhill between walls. Turn left at a track junction to reach a road near **Stonebeck Gate Farm**.

Turn left up the road to reach a farmhouse at **Fairy Cross Plain**. Turn right through a gate, as signposted public bridleway, and head across a field to reach the only other gate in view. Go through and bear right up to another gateway. Follow a grooved path across the flank of a prominent pointed hill, continuing across a

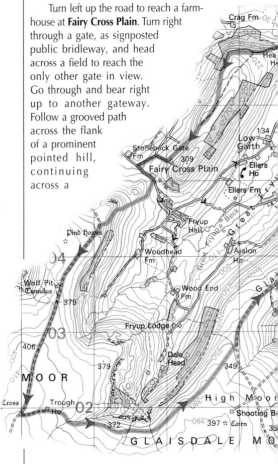

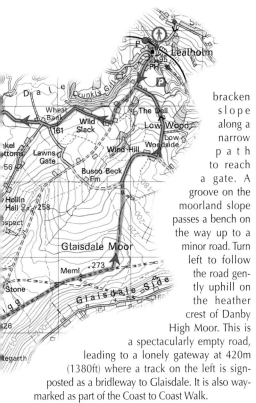

bracken slope along a narrow path to reach a gate. A groove on the moorland slope passes a bench on the way up to a minor road. Turn left to follow the road gently uphill on the heather crest of Danby High Moor. This is a spectacularly empty road, leading to a lonely gateway at 420m (1380ft) where a track on the left is signposted as a bridleway to Glaisdale. It is also waymarked as part of the Coast to Coast Walk.

Follow a clear track across the heather moor and pass the stout little stone building of **Trough House**. Keep following the clear track around the head of Great Fryup Dale, descending gently before climbing gently. This leads over **Glaisdale Moor**, at around 380m (1245ft), reaching a gate and a minor road. Turn left along the road and enjoy views down into Glaisdale. The road crosses a gentle dip on the moorland crest, then climbs gently. When the road bends left, leave it and follow a track straight ahead along **Glaisdale Rigg**, at 326m (1070ft).

Trough House is a lonely shooting hut situated up on Danby High Moor

The track is broad and clear and runs down into a gentle dip on the moorland crest. Note a stone marker on the left where 'Gisbro' and 'Whitby Road' can be discerned among the carvings, although other names are indistinct. Avoid other tracks on either side, and follow the main track as it climbs gently uphill and downhill on the slopes of **Glaisdale Moor**. A public bridleway marker points left up a path that is well marked by stone uprights. Follow it across the moorland crest, and it eventually leads down to a road. Turn right to follow the road across a cattle grid, then later turn left as signposted for Lealholm near **Wind Hill**. The road drops steeply and bends left, and there is also a short climb to a junction. Turn right downhill and cross the bridge over the River Esk to return to the village of **Lealholm**, and either take a break there or walk back up the path to the railway station.

WALK 35

Glaisdale Rigg, Egton High Moor and Egton Bridge

Start/finish	Glaisdale Railway Station, Eskdale, NZ 783 055
Distance	20km (12½ miles)
Total ascent/descent	500m (1640ft)
Time	6hrs 30mins
Terrain	A long, tough walk that follows quiet roads and clear tracks at first; the path that descends into Glaisdale needs care and is rather vague; other moorland paths are clear, but the high moors are exposed
Maps	OS Landranger 94; OS Explorer OL27 North
Refreshments	Arncliffe Arms at Glaisdale; Horseshoe Hotel at Egton Bridge
Transport	Northern trains serve Glaisdale and Egton Bridge from Whitby and Middlesbrough

There are high moorland roads alongside and around the head of Glaisdale, so a high-level circuit might be better made on a bicycle than on foot. Walkers would probably prefer to climb alongside Glaisdale, then drop down into the head of the dale and climb up the other side to appreciate its quiet charms. To avoid the road on the other side of the dale, it is better to follow a clear and obvious path across Egton High Moor before eventually descending to Egton Bridge. There are railway stations at Glaisdale and Egton Bridge, but there is also an opportunity to link both places using a road and a footpath.

Leave Glaisdale Railway Station and turn right up the road to the Arncliffe Arms, which offers food, drink and accommodation. Turn right downhill to follow the road near the river, then climb steeply up into **Glaisdale** village. Turn right to walk up High Terrace through the rest of the village, passing the village shop. Turn left at the top of the road, at a triangular green, to go up Hall Lane. The tarmac expires at a gate and a stony track leads out on to heathery **Glaisdale Moor**. Simply follow the broad clear track uphill, avoiding other tracks and paths to either side, and cross a dip on the moorland slopes.

Note a stone marker on the right, where 'Gisbro' and 'Whitby Road' can be discerned among the carvings, although other names are indistinct. Follow the track up **Glaisdale Rigg** to the top at 326m (1070ft), but stop just short of a tarmac road. Turn left along and down a path marked as a bridleway, reaching a small brick structure. Don't be in too much of a hurry to drop down into Glaisdale, but drift to the right along a vague path through bracken and bilberry. Head towards a drystone wall, then turn left downhill on a short, steep slope of bracken. Go through a little gate and walk down through fields and another couple of small gates to reach a road junction.

Walk down from the junction, across a bridge, and follow the road past **Yew Grange**, then pass a house with a little orchard nearby. Walk down the road to cross another beck, then up the road and round the back of some houses at Mountain Ash Farm. Turn right as signposted for a public bridleway, up a rough-pasture field and through a gate. Bend right and left, passing close to a forest, then away from the forest and up a moorland slope to a gate. Follow a rugged path over a heather moor that becomes easier and passes a stone-walled enclosure in a gentle dip at Wintergill.

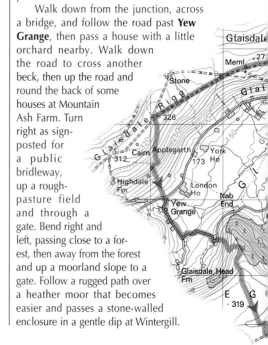

Follow a track up to a road, then turn left to follow the road alongside the forest of **Wintergill Plantation**.

Turn right to leave the road along a moorland track signposted as a public footpath. The track runs almost level at 320m (1050ft) over heathery **Egton High Moor**. There is a view of a pond off to the right, but keep following the clear track, which runs gently downhill over heather and bilberry to pass a lonesome pine tree. Note how the track appears to head for a portion of the sea around distant Whitby, but suddenly swings right to land on a minor road on **Murk Mire Moor**. Turn left to follow the road, passing a public footpath signpost as well as a prominent stone upright.

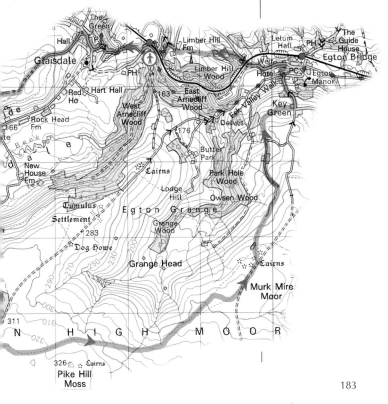

Black clouds pile up in the sky over the bleak and barren Egton High Moor

Turn left at a public bridleway signpost and follow a path through a groove on the heather moor. Cross a path and forge through bracken while following a rather wet and boggy path to reach a gate. Walk straight ahead, following a path across a rough pasture. Go through another gate and keep straight ahead, then later a grassy track swings left downhill. Follow it through the farmyard at Swang Farm, then follow the access track down and away from the farm.

When the access track turns right uphill, turn left to leave it and follow a short, overgrown grassy track flanked by trees to reach a gate. Walk past the left-hand side of a barn as signposted along a footpath, and continue along a grassy path flanked by trees and bushes, including plenty of holly. The path becomes a clear track that leads to a road at **Key Green**. Turn left down the road, where the Horseshoe Hotel at the bottom offers food, drink and accommodation. There are two sets of stepping stones across the River Esk between the hotel and the village of **Egton Bridge**. ◀ There are toilets in the village, as well as a railway station for those who wish to cut the route short and save walking the last 2.5km (1½ miles).

If the river is flowing too high, follow the road round to the village and cross a nearby bridge.

To continue with the walk, leave Egton Bridge by road, walking upstream alongside the river, where a placid stretch is held behind a **weir**. The road later veers away from the river and climbs beneath a railway arch, passing Broom House. Watch for a step-stile on the left, then follow a woodland fence uphill. Cross a dip and walk up to a stile to enter a stand of conifers, then climb further uphill. Exit from the trees and walk alongside a field, then cross a stile and continue straight along a track. Keep to the left of all the buildings at **Limber Hill Farm**. Turn right to reach a road bend, then turn left to walk down the road. To avoid the lower part of the road, turn left over a step-stile signposted as a public footpath. Cross a field and go down a steep and narrow woodland path. This leads straight on to the slender stone arch of Beggar's Bridge. Cross over this, rather than the adjacent road bridge, then follow the road under a railway arch. Simply turn right to finish back at **Glaisdale Railway Station**.

The slender stone arch of Beggar's Bridge near Glaisdale station

THE EASTERN MOORS

The Whinstone Ridge has been quarried and removed (Walk 38)

THE EASTERN MOORS

Many would claim that the Eastern Moors are part of the High Moors, but there is a distinct change in the moorlands as walkers progress eastwards: they dwindle in height, and although they still look broad, bleak and barren, forestry and cultivation have made great inroads into them. The peculiar pyramidal radar site at RAF Fylingdales is an abiding feature in this part of the North York Moors – a structure as incongruous as the monstrous 'golf ball' radomes that preceded it.

Drawing a line between the High Moors and the Eastern Moors could be done in a number of ways. The deep-cleft gorge of Newtondale, through which the North Yorkshire Moors Railway runs, is an obvious choice, and the busy A169 is another, but for the purposes of this guidebook the dividing line is Wheeldale. You could regard the low sprawling moorland of Simon Howe as part of the High Moors, but its character fits more into the Eastern Moors mould, and as it is traversed from Goathland, it has more in common with other walks in this section of the guidebook.

Goathland featured in the popular *Heartbeat* TV series, and of the six walks in this area, four are centred on that lovely village. Goathland is the starting point for a walk over Simon Howe, returning through Wheeldale. The Historic Rail Trail passes through the village on its way to Grosmont, where walkers can keep the theme in full steam by enjoying a ride on the North Yorkshire Moors Railway. Two more walks head eastwards on to the broad moorland slopes, one climbing uphill to take a close look at a curious geological feature known as Whinstone Ridge, and the other running high along the crest of Lilla Howe. The moorlands around Lilla Howe are so extensive that another walk tackles the slopes from Harwood Dale. The final offering in this section is a varied valley walk from Sleights.

There is actually one further walk in this area, and that is the last route in this guidebook, where the Lyke Wake Walk takes an astonishingly direct line across the moors to finish high above the coast at Ravenscar.

WALK 36

Goathland, Simon Howe, Wheeldale and Mallyan Spout

Start/finish	Mallyan Spout Hotel, Goathland, NZ 827 007
Distance	14.5km (9 miles)
Total ascent/descent	260m (855ft)
Time	5hrs
Terrain	A moderate walk along good moorland tracks and paths, with one vague stretch before the route continues along forest tracks; fiddly field paths give way to an awkward, bouldery, muddy walk along a wooded riverside path
Maps	OS Landranger 94; OS Explorers OL27 South and OL27 North
Refreshments	Mallyan Spout Hotel and other places down the road in Goathland
Transport	Yorkshire Coastliner buses serve Goathland from Whitby and Pickering; North Yorkshire Moors Railway serves Goathland from Grosmont and Pickering

Simon Howe is a broad moorland, but it is not particularly high or extensive. However, it does stand somewhat in isolation, rising between Wheeldale and Newtondale, offering extensive views around Fylingdales Moor and the High Moors. An ascent is easily accomplished from Goathland, then moorland paths and forest tracks link with the ancient 'Roman' road at Wheeldale. A rather awkward, bouldery, muddy and slippery walk alongside West Beck leads to the delicate waterfall of Mallyan Spout, from where the return to Goathland rises up a long flight of steps.

Start at the top end of Goathland village, beside the church and Mallyan Spout Hotel. Just beyond the road junction and mini-roundabout is the Jubilee Tree and Pinfold. Keep left of the tree to walk up a grassy path that rises from a noticeboard. The path becomes clearer as it climbs over a grassy moorland rise to reach a pool known as The Tarn on a gap. Turn right along a path to walk close to it, then swing left uphill away from it.

A series of parallel paths rise gradually on a heather moorland slope, so choose one to your liking. You will reach a cairn on a grassy bump where you will see another cairn nearby, but don't go to it. Together these bumps are known as the Two Howes. Keep to the clearest path ahead along the moorland crest of **Two Howes Rigg**. The ground can be wet and muddy in places, but there is always drier footing nearby. The path links with another bridleway and reaches a cairn on top of **Simon Howe**, although the summit trig point at 260m (853ft) is further away and doesn't have to be visited. Enjoy views around the higher moors, whose near-horizontal lines are broken only by the strange radar pyramid at RAF Fylingdales.

Turn right to follow a clear path heading westwards away from the cairn. Parallel paths on the heather moor can be wet and muddy in places. You will then reach a firm, dry gritstone edge overlooking **Wheeldale Lodge**, formerly a youth hostel. ▶

An obvious short cut across Wheeldale is possible here.

Turn left to follow a clear path and keep to the clearest path at junctions with other paths on heathery Howl Moor. Stay well away from an isolated hut, but watch carefully as it is necessary to turn right along a rather vague path, which eventually reaches two footbridges at

189

Blawath Beck near a forest. Walk up to a forest track and turn right, then keep right at junctions with other tracks around Gale Hill Rigg, following the main track to a gate leading out of the forest. Turn right down a road to reach a culvert and ford on Wheeldale Beck, then follow the road uphill. Branch right to cross a stile beside an information board and follow the **Roman Road**.

> The ancient **Wheeldale Road** is also known as Wade's Causeway. A giant by the name of Wade is said to have built the road for his wife Bell to herd her sheep along. For a long time it was assumed to be a Roman road, although some archaeologists now doubt this and suggest that it may be late Roman or even pre-Roman.

Follow the old road across the moor, perhaps walking alongside as the surface is rather rough and bouldery. Pass a gate and ladder stile to follow an even

Walkers follow the rough and stony course of the Wheeldale 'Roman' Road

rougher stretch downhill. When you reach another information board, drift right and left as marked, down through fields to continue down a clear track. Before reaching a flat field, turn left and cross a stile on the right, then cross a footbridge over Wheeldale Gill near a ford. Turn left to follow a track signposted as a bridleway, screened by trees, straight up from the ford. Bear right on the way up and go through a gate to pass in front of **Hazel Head** farm. Follow the access road away from the farm, then watch for a public bridleway signpost beside a small gate on the right. Turn right and walk downhill to go through another gate, then turn left. Turn right at the next gate, then left at the bottom of a field to follow a woodland path downhill. Go through a tiny meadow and pass a house, then cross a long footbridge over **West Beck**. Walk up to a concrete access road and turn right up to a minor road. Turn left down the road, then turn right at a bridge to follow a path.

Be warned that the riverside path is rough and bouldery, and slippery tree roots are exposed in places. When the path becomes wet and muddy, it needs even more care. The rugged wooded valley through which West Beck flows is like a jungle in places. It is better to follow a parallel alternative path along a bracken-clad brow above the river and woods and descend steps later to rejoin the riverside path. The route crosses two footbridges before wooden steps lead up to **Mallyan Spout**, which is a delicate, feathery curtain of water spilling down a mossy face. Continue along the riverside path, heading downstream to a prominent path junction. ▶ Turn right up a flight of 180 steps to return to the Mallyan Spout Hotel.

Mallyan Spout is a delicate little waterfall near Goathland

The path continuing downstream to Beck Hole on Walk 37 is very pleasant.

WALK 37

*Rail Trail from Moorgates to
Goathland and Grosmont*

Start	Moorgates, near Goathland, SE 844 994
Finish	Grosmont Railway Station, NZ 828 052
Distance	7.5km (4¾ miles)
Total ascent	20m (65ft)
Total descent	130m (425ft)
Time	2hrs 30mins
Terrain	Easy walking along level, firm dry tracks in a valley and woodlands
Maps	OS Landranger 94; OS Explorer OL27 North
Refreshments	Pubs, restaurants and tearooms at Goathland and Grosmont
Transport	Yorkshire Coastliner buses serve Goathland from Whitby and Pickering; North Yorkshire Moors Railway serves Goathland and Grosmont from Pickering; Northern trains serve Grosmont from Whitby and Middlesbrough

The North Yorkshire Moors Railway is a well-known attraction, with steam trains running between Pickering, Levisham, Goathland and Grosmont. The line from Pickering to Whitby was constructed by George Stephenson and opened in 1836. The first passengers travelled in horse-drawn carriages as steam trains were unable to use a 1:5 (20%) incline at Beck Hole. When George Hudson bought the line, he diverted the track away from Beck Hole in 1865, so that steam engines could use the line. However, a branch line to Beck Hole was maintained, and summer services from Whitby operated up until 1914. The old trackbed now offers a short and easy low-level linear walk known as the Rail Trail.

If this is not possible, start in Goathland and omit the first 2km (1¼ miles) of the walk.

To enjoy the entire length of the old railway track, start by being dropped off at Moorgates, between Goathland and the A169 at Eller Beck. ◄ Moorgates was once a level crossing and the road below the houses passes arches on both the former and current railway lines. Start just

The old railway trackbed to Goathland is joined at Moor Crossing at Moorgates

below the house and go through a white gate to follow the old trackbed. This is broad and clear and now serves as an access track leading to **Sadler House**. Go through a gate beside the farm and follow a grassy stretch of the trackbed that is flanked by trees. Go through another gate to continue along the old line. **Abbot's House Farm** campsite spreads on both sides of the trackbed later.

The old line is now the access track for the farm and runs straight ahead, still flanked by trees, to reach **Goathland**. Pop out on to the road beside the Goathland Hotel. ▶

This was the Aidensfield Hotel during filming for the Heartbeat TV series, while across the road the Aidensfield Garage operates as a souvenir shop.

193

Turn right to pass the hotel, then turn left along Mill Green Way and follow it to a road in another part of the village. Turn left along the road, then almost immediately right as signposted for the Rail Trail to Grosmont. The level grassy old line begins to slope downhill and crosses a road; the line was a twin track, and while carriages were lowered up and down one line, heavy water barrels were hauled up and down the other line to counterbalance them. Walk down the old trackbed into dense woodlands in a valley. The trees thin out at a gateway, and the route continues past Incline Cottage where the old line levels out, then pass a small community orchard. Cross a footbridge and pass the site of **Beck Hole Station**.

The trackbed continues, sometimes with views on either side and sometimes through woodlands that obscure views. Cross two footbridges mounted on the original supports that carried the old railway across the **Murk Esk**. After following the line through fields with more open views, cross another footbridge, then the line runs

mostly through woods. Pass a stone house and continue through a small wooded cutting at **Spring Wood**. Pass between a row of houses and a converted chapel at **Esk Valley**, then the trackbed becomes quite broad and cindery, and gradually runs close to the current railway line. Look along the line to see the engine sheds on the North York Moors Railway, although there is no access to them from this side.

Follow a gravel path uphill and go through a gate. Turn right, crossing high above a tunnel that carries the railway, then turn left through a gate and follow a broad, stony woodland path downhill alongside St Matthew's Church. The village of **Grosmont** is directly ahead, but first it is worth turning left to follow a path straight through a tunnel to see the engine sheds. ▶ The walk finishes at **Grosmont Railway Station**, but note that there are actually two stations side by side. One is operated by the North York Moors Railway, and the other by Northern, connecting with Whitby and Middlesbrough.

A level trackbed follows the Murk Esk through a pleasant valley

The tunnel was cut between 1833 and 1835 under the direction of George Stephenson and is thought to be the world's first railway tunnel.

195

WALK 38
Goathland, Sleights Moor and Whinstone Ridge

Start/finish	Goathland Railway Station, NZ 836 013
Distance	6.5km (4 miles)
Total ascent/descent	200m (655ft)
Time	2hrs
Terrain	A moderate short walk where moorland paths are fairly good, while low-level paths and tracks are clear throughout
Maps	OS Landranger 94; OS Explorer OL27 North
Refreshments	Pubs, restaurants and tearooms at Goathland
Transport	Yorkshire Coastliner buses serve Goathland from Whitby and Pickering; North Yorkshire Moors Railway serves Goathland from Grosmont and Pickering

Running across Goathland Moor and beyond, a linear feature called the Whinstone Ridge is marked on maps, but there is no ridge. Instead, walkers find a deep trough cut into the moorland, with piles of rubble being colonised by vegetation. There was once a ridge – a hard upstanding dyke of basalt, also known as the Cleveland Dyke, which was squeezed in a molten state into surrounding bedrock almost 60 million years ago. It was quarried away for roadstone, being highly prized in an area that generally features only crumbling sandstone, shale and limestone. Climb high above Goathland to see this awesome gash on the moors, then drop down to Darnholm on the way back to Goathland.

Start from Goathland Railway Station and climb 36 steps straight up from the station platform on the opposite side of the track to the village. When you reach a junction, only a short way uphill, turn right along a level grassy path, then turn left up a narrow grassy path. The vegetation changes to heather as you gain height and reach a square-cut pool on the moorland, which is an old reservoir. Continue straight uphill and the path gradually

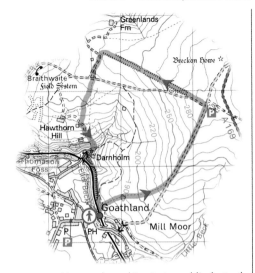

converges with a road, reaching it at a public footpath signpost. Turn left to walk up the road, and use the verges for safety's sake if there is any amount of traffic. Walk as far as a road junction and turn left, as signposted for Green End and Beck Hole.

Immediately after turning left, step off the road to the right and follow a path through a deep groove scored down the moorland slope. This was where the Whinstone Ridge ran before it was quarried. Walk in the bottom of the cut, although later it might be better to keep to the moorland on one side or the other if the floor of the cut becomes rough and stony. Keep following the quarried entrenchment over Sleights Moor until you reach enclosures around fields near **Greenlands Farm**. Turn left along a road and follow it to a junction. Cross over the road to continue as signposted along a public footpath.

Follow a clear and grassy path down a slope of heather. Keep left down a track, then keep left again at a gate, following a path that steepens as it drops into a valley. Go down flights of steps on a partially wooded slope and cross a footbridge at the bottom to reach

Darnholm is a pleasant little huddle of houses situated beside Eller Beck

a track. Turn right along the track to reach a ford at **Darnholm**, but there is no need to cross it. Simply turn left to walk a short way upstream beside Eller Beck, then turn left again up a steep flight of stone steps above the railway line. Continue alongside a drystone wall, across a moorland slope, until you reach the steps you climbed earlier in the day, which drop back on to the platform at **Goathland Railway Station**.

WALK 39

*Goathland, Eller Beck, Lilla Howe
and Goathland Moor*

Start/finish	Goathland Railway Station, NZ 836 013
Distance	16km (10 miles)
Total ascent/descent	240m (790ft)
Time	5hrs 30mins
Terrain	A tough walk starting with a clear track and road followed by clear moorland paths and tracks; the route follows a road and a vague path on the descent, and the high moors are exposed.
Maps	OS Landranger 94; OS Explorers OL27 North and South
Refreshments	Pubs, restaurants and tearooms at Goathland.
Transport	Yorkshire Coastliner buses serve Goathland from Whitby and Pickering; North Yorkshire Moors Railway serves Goathland from Grosmont and Pickering.

This route starts in gentle pastures around Goathland and climbs on to bleak and barren Goathland Moor and Fylingdales Moor. Apart from the dominance of RAF Fylingdales and its strange central pyramid, walkers will spot a number of stone uprights that have been planted along the crest of the moorland over the centuries. Lilla Cross is undoubtedly one of the most striking moorland markers, but the less well-known examples are just as interesting in their own right. The busy A169 is an intrusion into the wilds, completely bisecting this route, and care is needed when crossing or following it.

Start from Goathland Railway Station and walk up into the village to reach the Goathland Hotel. Turn left beside the hotel along a clear track signposted as a public bridleway. The track is flanked by trees and the **Abbot's House Farm** campsite spreads away on both sides. Keep straight ahead along the track, which is the trackbed of an old railway, and go through a gate to follow a grassy stretch. Go through another gate beside **Sadler House** and

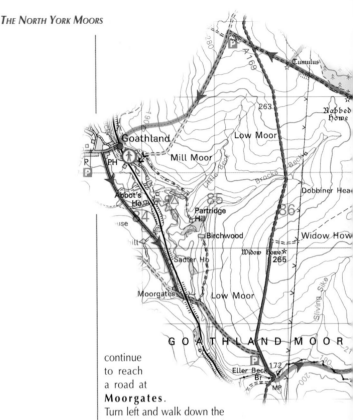

continue
to reach
a road at
Moorgates.
Turn left and walk down the
road, passing under a railway
arch and crossing Eller Beck. Follow the road up on to
Goathland Moor to join the busy A169, and turn right to
follow this road, walking with care along the right-hand
side, facing the traffic, to cross **Eller Beck Bridge**.

Turn left to leave the road and follow a track that is
clearly marked as running on to MOD property – part of
RAF Fylingdales. Go through a gate and walk beneath a
pylon line to the end of the track. Keep to the left-hand side
of a fence to continue, following a path across a boggy
area full of bog myrtle. The path aligns itself to **Little Eller
Beck** and pulls away from the fence. A line of metal posts

have been planted all the way up the heather moorland slope, and it is best to keep to the left of them. It can be muddy underfoot in places, but later you will reach a firm gravel track and a left turn leads past a few trees to a gate. Go through the gate and cross another track, walking straight ahead up a more rugged path on a heather slope. Cross a rough track then aim for the **cross on Lilla Howe**, at 292m (958ft). Although of no great height, this moorland top offers extensive views through the heart of the North York Moors.

Of all the crosses dotted around the North York Moors National Park, **Lilla Cross** is reckoned to be the oldest. It stands on a Bronze Age burial mound and was erected to commemorate Lilla, a minister to King Edwin of Northumbria whose intervention during an assassination attempt on the king led to his own death in AD626. The cross was removed for safe keeping when the moors were used for military training, then later replanted.

Walk back a short way downhill and turn right along the rugged track to reach an intersection of tracks. Turn left and walk up a gentle incline to **Louven Howe**. A heathery mound is crowned with a stone stump and a trig point at 299m (981ft). Continue along the track and cross over a broader track to go straight ahead through a gate. Walk gently along and down a rugged moorland track along a broad heathery crest; there is always a fence to the right. The track then climbs very gently uphill, passing **Ann's Cross** on a tumulus. Keep walking along the track

The route crosses Eller Beck Bridge close to the MOD property at RAF Fylingdales

and go through a gate where the twin heathery humps of **Foster Howes** lie to the left.

The track continues and the fence is now on the left-hand side. However, the track swings right, away from the fence, then left, running gradually down **York Cross Rigg** to level out beside a forest. It can be muddy as the track follows the course of **Whinstone Ridge**, a dyke of igneous rock intruded into the bedrock of the moors. Pass the heathery hump of **Robbed Howe** and climb gently to pass beneath a pylon line, also passing a bridleway signpost where a tumulus on the right bears a couple of stone uprights. Continue gently uphill to the busy **A169** at a lay-by. Cross the road with care and go through a gate to continue along a short grassy track, over a heathery rise, to reach a quieter moorland road.

Turn left to walk down the road, on the right-hand side, and later watch out for a public footpath signpost pointing down to the right. A path runs downhill, reaching a square-cut pool, which turns out to be an old reservoir. Continue further down the path, through heather, reaching a broader path on a grassy slope. Turn right for just a short way, then left to go down 36 steps to land back on the platform at **Goathland Railway Station**.

Moorlands stretch towards the sea in this view from Lilla Howe

WALK 40

Chapel Farm, Lilla Howe and Jugger Howe Beck

Start/finish	Chapel Farm, SE 952 967
Distance	17km (10½ miles)
Total ascent/descent	300m (985ft)
Time	5hrs 30mins
Terrain	A tough walk where rugged woodland paths quickly give way to clear farm tracks and moorland tracks; paths through the valley towards the end are quite rugged too
Maps	OS Landranger 94 or 101; OS Explorer OL27 South
Refreshments	Grainary Tearoom off-route in Harwood Dale
Transport	None to Chapel Farm, although regular Arriva buses run along the nearby A171 between Whitby and Scarborough

This route explores a quiet part of Fylingdales Moor, the access point being Chapel Farm on the Helwath road in Harwood Dale. The route passes through Castlebeck Wood and climbs gradually through huge fields that have been wrested from the moorland slopes. A fine clear track can be followed on to the higher moors, even to the extent of visiting Lilla Cross on Lilla Howe. The return route wanders gently down another moorland track, passing Burn Howe and leading into the rugged valley drained by Jugger Howe Beck. The valley leads back into the woods below Chapel Farm.

Start at Chapel Farm in Harwood Dale, where a signpost beside the road reads 'Bridleway to Lilla'. The path is muddy as it descends through nettles, continuing down a field, turning right through a gate where the Woodland Trust welcomes walkers to **Castlebeck Wood**. Walk down into the woods and cross a footbridge over **Jugger Howe Beck**. Walk uphill and swing left up a muddy groove to reach a small gate at the top of the wooded slope. Turn right through fields and walk towards a building at **Park Hill**. Pass through a small gate as marked, keep well to the left of the building and turn left up its access road.

Lilla Cross may be the oldest of all the moorland crosses in the North York Moors

This stands at 292m (958ft), and although of no great height, there are extensive views through the heart of the North York Moors.

When the road bends left, turn right through a gate and walk alongside a field. At the end of the field turn left to go through a small gate to walk alongside another field. Go through another gate and turn right along a clear track that leads away from **Riverhead Farm**.

The track runs through huge fields and passes a pool with a few trees around it. Keep straight ahead at a gate and walk alongside one final field at **Brown Hill**. Go through a gate and follow a track out on to heather moorland. The track is broad and clear, rising gently uphill. There is a dip later where the ground can be muddy and rutted. After rising from this point, note a track joining from the right at a boulder, as you will return here later. For now, keep straight ahead up the track, then branch left up a lesser path to reach the prominent **cross on Lilla Howe**. ◄

Walk back down the path from Lilla Howe, keeping right along a track to return to the junction with the boulder, which was passed earlier. Branch left along a track that can be rough and stony as well as muddy when wet. It is clear and obvious as it descends gently over Fylingdales Moor, passing a cairn on a mound known as **Burn Howe**. The track becomes a narrow path, but remains clear to follow, then becomes steep and stone-paved as it drops towards **Jugger Howe Beck**. Cross a footbridge over the beck and turn right. Follow a path uphill, but watch for a marker pointing right and follow a lesser path in that direction.

The path crosses wet and boggy ground using duckboards. It then traverses bracken, heather and bog myrtle slopes before it begins to climb, later crossing a footbridge. Turn right and follow very vague paths along a brow overlooking the valley. If the paths are difficult to locate, try walking from one solitary tree to another. Watch carefully to spot where the path descends a slope of bracken and reaches a footbridge over Helwath Beck. Cross over and keep right to walk downstream alongside

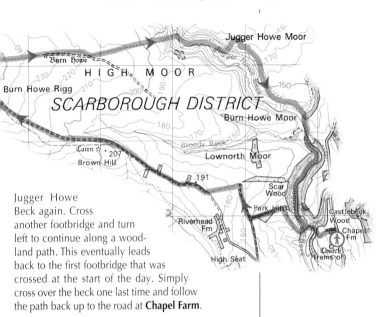

Jugger Howe
Beck again. Cross
another footbridge and turn
left to continue along a woodland path. This eventually leads
back to the first footbridge that was
crossed at the start of the day. Simply
cross over the beck one last time and follow
the path back up to the road at **Chapel Farm**.

A boardwalk path runs close to Jugger Howe Beck

WALK 41

Sleights, Ugglebarnby, Falling Foss and Littlebeck

Start/finish	Sleights Railway Station, NZ 868 081
Distance	12.5km (7¾ miles)
Total ascent/descent	270m (885ft)
Time	4hrs
Terrain	A moderate walk along a fairly fiddly selection of paths and tracks that run through fields, alongside moorland, through woods, more fields and along riversides
Maps	OS Landranger 94; OS Explorer OL27 North
Refreshments	Plough Inn and Salmon Leap in Sleights; teas at Falling Foss
Transport	Northern trains, Arriva buses and Yorkshire Coastliner buses serve Sleights from Whitby

This is essentially a valley walk, although it does climb high above Sleights and reaches the fringes of Ugglebarnby Moor. After dropping back down into a wooded valley, the route includes a glimpse of Falling Foss, which is a gentle, slender waterfall most of the time. The woods between the waterfall and Littlebeck are managed as a nature reserve. Various paths are linked together to form a route that runs roughly parallel to Little Beck all the way back to Sleights. The route is structured from the railway station, but it could be covered just as easily from bus services in the village.

Start from Sleights Railway Station and walk along Lowdale Lane, avoiding a turning for Echo Hill. The lane later runs beside Iburndale Beck, then turns right away from a bowling green. Walk up the road, then turn left at Whin Green, which is signposted as a public footpath. At the end of the road, turn left to cross a narrow footbridge and follow a paved and grassy path to a house. Keep to the left of the main buildings as marked, then drift right uphill. Watch out on the right for a footbridge and cross it, then climb steeply to locate a path on a wooded slope.

Follow the path alongside a field and pass a couple of gates to reach a road. Turn left up the road towards the village of **Ugglebarnby**, but just before reaching a road junction turn right as signposted along Tom Bell Lane. Later, turn left up a broader track and continue up between buildings at **Dean Hall** to reach a minor road.

Turn right down the road, then branch left as signposted along a public bridleway, before reaching **Hempsyke Hall**, following a path into woods. Keep straight ahead until forced to turn left uphill by a wall. Continue through woods and out on to a heather moorland dotted with conifers. Keep to the path alongside **Ugglebarnby Moor** to reach a farm. Follow the access track away, but watch out on the right for an unmarked path short-cutting to a nearby minor road. ▶ Turn right down the road, then left as signposted public bridleway. This is overgrown with bracken until it reaches a farm access track near **Thorn Hill**. The path is clearer, and later reaches a house. Turn right down a minor road.

If the short-cut is missed, the access road leads to the minor road anyway.

Falling Foss is seen briefly in a well-wooded valley

The road runs down into woods at the Falling Foss Forest Nature Reserve. Keep right of a car park and walk down a steep track to cross a stone-arched bridge to reach a house offering teas. Cross a footbridge to reach a viewpoint for the waterfall of **Falling Foss**. Keep to the right to follow the clearest path up and across the wooded valley sides, reaching a path junction where a left turn is signposted for Littlebeck. Turn left and follow the path down to The Hermitage, which is a rock outcrop with a shelter carved into it. Continue straight ahead and down stone steps, crossing muddy patches, slippery tree roots and boulders, into **Little Beck Wood**, which is managed as a nature reserve by the Yorkshire Wildlife Trust. Some stretches of the

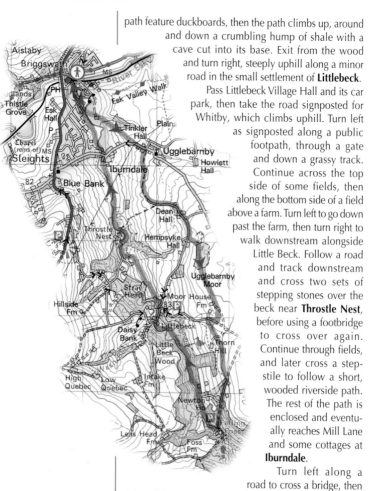

path feature duckboards, then the path climbs up, around and down a crumbling hump of shale with a cave cut into its base. Exit from the wood and turn right, steeply uphill along a minor road in the small settlement of **Littlebeck**.

Pass Littlebeck Village Hall and its car park, then take the road signposted for Whitby, which climbs uphill. Turn left as signposted along a public footpath, through a gate and down a grassy track. Continue across the top side of some fields, then along the bottom side of a field above a farm. Turn left to go down past the farm, then turn right to walk downstream alongside Little Beck. Follow a road and track downstream and cross two sets of stepping stones over the beck near **Throstle Nest**, before using a footbridge to cross over again. Continue through fields, and later cross a step-stile to follow a short, wooded riverside path. The rest of the path is enclosed and eventually reaches Mill Lane and some cottages at **Iburndale**.

Turn left along a road to cross a bridge, then right to follow a short track between houses. This gives way to a narrow path, which soon broadens and runs alongside Iburndale Beck. When you reach a tarmac road, simply turn right and left by road to walk back to **Sleights Railway Station** to complete the walk.

THE CLEVELAND COAST

A path climbs from a beach at Hob Holes on to the cliffs near Kettleness (Walk 42)

THE CLEVELAND COAST

By the time the North York Moors National Park reaches the coast, the moorlands have already given way to gentle cultivated countryside cleft by wooded valleys. The only place of any size is the town of Whitby, a former whaling town that has since turned its hand to tourism, which sits at the point where the River Esk spills into the North Sea. There are several villages too, including lovely Staithes, Runswick Bay, Kettleness, Sandsend, Robin Hood's Bay and the peculiar 'failed resort' of Ravenscar. Between each settlement there are fine cliffs, and because of the Jurassic geology, wealth of fossils, abundant wildlife and abiding historical interest of these dramatic cliffs, the whole coastline has been designated the Cleveland Heritage Coast. A peculiar weather feature along the coast is the dense fog, or 'roak', that sometimes blows in from the sea.

After leaving the moors, the Cleveland Way enjoys a splendid romp along cliff paths all the way from Saltburn-on-Sea to Scarborough and Filey, even including cliffs that lie outside the national park boundary, to get the most from the coast. Many visitors who enjoy good walks are familiar with the cliff coast, but not all of them realise that there is another walking route available a short way inland, running roughly parallel to the coast. A coastal railway once linked Scarborough with Whitby, Saltburn and beyond, but only the northern stretch survives as a mineral line. The rest of the line between Scarborough and Whitby has been retained as the Cinder Track walkway and cycleway, tying in with the coast path at various settlements along the way.

Five walks are described along the coast, and four of these make use of stretches of the old railway line (which operated from 1885 to 1965), so that a series of fine circular walks can be completed. On the first route walkers will barely notice the old line between Runswick Bay and Staithes, and the route uses the cliff coast path to link both charming villages. Another stretch of coastal path links Runswick Bay with Kettleness, returning along the old railway trackbed. The cliff coast walk from Whitby to Robin Hood's Bay is a short classic walk that uses the old line further inland, where it remains plain and obvious throughout. Similarly, the short coast walk from Robin Hood's Bay to Ravenscar returns along the line. Finally, the last walk follows a longer stretch of the old trackbed from Cloughton to Ravenscar, returning along the roller-coaster cliff path afterwards. Together these routes allow most of the Cleveland Coast to be explored, along with most of the Cinder Track further inland. Strong walkers can of course combine any two walks that share a common link and extend each day's explorations.

WALK 42

Runswick Bay, Hinderwell,
Staithes and Port Mulgrave

Start/finish	Runswick Bay Hotel, NZ 806 161
Distance	11.5km (7 miles)
Total ascent/descent	200m (655ft)
Time	3hrs 30mins
Terrain	Easy walking along clear roads, tracks and paths leading inland, with a couple of vague stretches; a clear cliff coast path closes the circuit
Maps	OS Landranger 94; OS Explorer OL27 North
Refreshments	Pubs at Hinderwell, Dalehouse and Port Mulgrave; pubs, restaurants and cafés at Staithes and Runswick Bay
Transport	Regular Arriva buses link Runswick Bay, Hinderwell and Staithes with Whitby, Guisborough and Middlesbrough

The coastal walk between the lovely little harbour at Staithes and the amazing stack of houses at Runswick Bay is fairly popular, but few walkers venture inland, where an interesting wooded valley of The Dales is located. This walk starts at Runswick Bay and heads inland first, bypassing Hinderwell to go down through The Dales, then climbs over to Staithes to explore the crooked little harbour and its associations with the young James Cook. Afterwards, a fine cliff coast walk leads to Port Mulgrave, an old ironstone port that was serviced by tunnels from Grinkle, far inland. Another fine stretch of cliff coast returns walkers to Runswick Bay.

Start at the Runswick Bay Hotel and follow Hinderwell Lane, which is signposted for Hinderwell and has a pavement alongside throughout its length. When you reach the first houses at **Hinderwell**, turn left as signposted along a public footpath and walk alongside a field to reach the A174. Turn right along the road, then take the first turning on the left, which is Browns Terrace. Walk off the end of the tarmac road to follow a track known

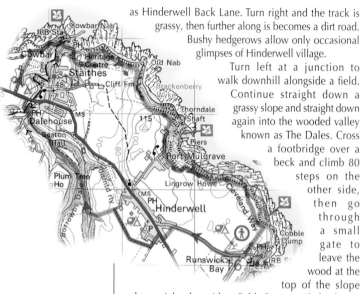

as Hinderwell Back Lane. Turn right and the track is grassy, then further along is becomes a dirt road. Bushy hedgerows allow only occasional glimpses of Hinderwell village.

Turn left at a junction to walk downhill alongside a field. Continue straight down a grassy slope and straight down again into the wooded valley known as The Dales. Cross a footbridge over a beck and climb 80 steps on the other side, then go through a small gate to leave the wood at the top of the slope and turn right alongside a field. Cross a stile back into the wood and turn left, following a narrow path through dense woodland planted along a ridge beside **Borrowby Dale**. Watch for a yellow sign just to the left, which reads 'Oakridge Nature Reserve', and pass it. A clear path reaches a gate and you continue along a broad grassy swathe surrounded by woodland. Walk down a steep

Owl sculpture seen beside the path through Borrowby Dale

gravel path to a small caravan site and follow the access track away across a bridge. Walk down a concrete road to reach a bridge at **Dalehouse** and turn right along a road to reach the Fox and Hounds pub.

Turn left beside the pub to cross a narrow bridge where an old road has been blocked against traffic and is now very overgrown. Follow it uphill by swinging right, then cross the A174 with care. Turn left and walk on the right-hand side of the road, facing oncoming traffic for safety, while crossing a rise. Turn right along the access road for Cowbar Farm, and keep right of the farm to follow a path under an old stone railway arch in the fields beyond. Walk straight across a field to reach a minor road at **Cowbar**. Turn right to follow the road down to the charming, colourful village of **Staithes**. Cross a footbridge over the narrow harbour to reach the main part of the village.

The narrow natural harbour, with its protective projecting cliff face at Cowbar Nab, made **Staithes** an ideal retreat for fishermen, traders and smugglers. Latterly the higgledy-piggledy houses and narrow alleys have enchanted artists and photographers. For a thorough grounding in the history of this delightfully jumbled village, be sure to visit the Captain Cook & Staithes Heritage Centre. The teenage James Cook worked as an assistant to a Staithes shopkeeper called William Sanderson. The sea destroyed the original shop, but parts of it were incorporated into Captain Cook's Cottage. Cook stayed for only 18 months, then moved to Whitby to train as an apprentice seaman and embark on his seafaring career.

After crossing the footbridge over the harbour, walk up to a narrow cobbled street and turn left. You will reach the Cod & Lobster pub, which has been partially demolished by storms three times. Turn right up Church Street and pass Captain Cook's Cottage. Follow the stone-paved Cleveland Way even further uphill to leave the village, taking a last fond look back at the intriguing jumble of cottages.

The narrow and attractive harbour and higgledy piggledy houses at Staithes

Turn left, as signposted for Runswick Bay, to follow a clear path past a farm. Turn left as signposted along a broad grassy track flanked by fences. Turn right along the cliff tops and right again above the promontory of **Old Nab**, climbing steadily. Keep climbing uphill, almost to 100m (330ft) on Beacon Hill. You can follow the next road, Rosedale Lane, inland from **Port Mulgrave** to reach the Ship Inn tearoom for refreshments, otherwise stay on the route.

PORT MULGRAVE

Although the broken remains of a small harbour can be seen at Port Mulgrave, access from the tiny village is restricted. In fact, access to the harbour lies through underground tunnels originating far inland at the Grinkle ironstone mines, so there has never been a need for a road link from the village. Ironstone was later removed from Grinkle by rail, and as the tunnels were no longer needed, they were closed and the harbour fell into disuse by 1916.

The Cleveland Way is signposted off a corner of the road and along the top of the rugged slope known as Rosedale Cliffs. Go down and up flights of steps, then follow the path around **Lingrow Howe**, eventually reaching a small pond, then turn right inland to return to the **Runswick Bay Hotel**. There are bus stops nearby on Ellerby Lane, or the route could be extended immediately by embarking on Walk 43.

WALK 43

Runswick Bay, Kettleness and Goldsborough

Start/finish	Runswick Bay Hotel, NZ 806 161
Distance	12.5km (7¾ miles)
Total ascent/descent	200m (655ft)
Time	4hrs
Terrain	Easy walking, but the first part of the route is along a beach and is impassable at high tide; a cliff path gives way to paths inland, then an old railway trackbed starts firm and clear but becomes overgrown later
Maps	OS Landranger 94; OS Explorer OL27 North.
Refreshments	Pubs, restaurants and café at Runswick Bay; Fox and Hounds restaurant at Goldsborough
Transport	Regular Arriva buses link Runswick Bay with Whitby, Guisborough and Middlesbrough

The sandy beach walk around Runswick Bay is the only sandy beach in the whole guidebook, so make the most of it! A fine cliff walk continues around Kettleness, then the route heads inland to the little farming village of Goldsborough. After dropping back down to the village of Kettleness, the course of an old railway trackbed at first runs close to the coast, then swings inland in an enormous loop, crossing wooded valleys where views are more limited. This walk can be conveniently extended by linking with Walk 42.

Start at the Runswick Bay Hotel and follow the road past the Cliffemount Hotel, then walk down a narrow road closed to vehicles before continuing down to the beach at Runswick Bay. Note that onward progress might be blocked across **Runswick Sands** by very high tides, so time your arrival to avoid high water. Turn right to walk along the sandy beach, passing the blue-and-white Runswick Bay Sailing Club building at the far end. Continue past a crumbling cliff at **Hob Holes** to find a river valley cutting through flaky beds of shale. Head inland through this valley as marked, scrambling up crumbling slopes of shale. Climb a flight of 95 steps and then follow another flight of 160 steps up a bushy slope, out of the valley and along the top of High Cliff, at around 100m (330ft). (The disused railway line used for the return is only a short distance inland at this point.)

The cliff path is pushed inland a little by a small gully choked with bushes. Turn left to follow a track through the farming hamlet of **Kettleness**. Apart from the first white building, keep seawards of all other buildings to pick up the cliff path as marked later.

KETTLENESS

The bare, rugged headland of Kettle Ness was once worked for alum, jet and ironstone. The previous village of Kettleness slumped into the sea in 1829. There was no loss of life, since the slump was gradual and the inhabitants were safely loaded on to a ship that was waiting for a consignment of alum. The alum works were destroyed, along with the village, but the slump exposed more shale to be quarried, so a new works was built and operations began again within two years.

The rugged and crumbling cliffs at Kettleness

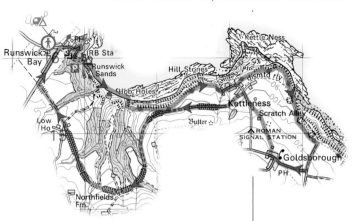

After following the grassy cliff-top path around the **Kettle Ness** headland, note that the disused railway is close to hand again. Watch it carefully to see it disappear into a tunnel. ▶ Keep following the cliff path onwards, but watch out for a vague track running uphill and inland and follow it to a road corner. Turn right along the road to reach the little village of **Goldsborough**, where you will find the Fox and Hounds, a sort of farmyard restaurant.

Continue straight along the road signposted for Kettleness, but turn right, as indicated by a public footpath signpost, through a farmyard and down an overgrown track. Veer slightly left across a large field of rough grazing, noting a mass of thistles on a hump where a **Roman Signal Station** was sited inn AD368. ▶ Cross a stile and walk down towards a chapel, then turn right down the road towards Kettleness. The first big building on the left is the old railway station; before reaching it, turn left to follow a clear track.

Continue along the old railway trackbed, which offers good views of the coast, at least while it runs near the cliffs – when the trackbed swings left inland, views become more restricted. Measure progress by ticking off four stone arches over the old line as the trackbed moves through bushy cuttings and has a grassy surface.

The tunnel, or tunnels, since there are actually two, was cut after the original coastal railway was lost in a cliff-fall.

Coastal signal stations were linked by lines of sight through Hartlepool, Hunt Cliff, Boulby, Goldsborough, Whitby, Ravenscar, Scarborough and Filey.

The last arch is followed by a broad and muddy track that passes close to **Low House**. Continue straight along another grassy stretch where the path narrows considerably among nettles and brambles. However, the old line quickly leads to a road, dropping on to it where a bridge has been demolished. This is Ellerby Lane and a right turn along it leads straight back to the **Runswick Bay Hotel**.

RUNSWICK BAY

This delightful little village is stacked up a steep slope facing a curved bay with a fine sandy beach. Despite its obvious beauty, the situation looks precarious. One night in 1664, when most of the villagers were attending a funeral wake, the houses started to slip into the sea. By morning every dwelling was in ruins, except, for some mysterious reason, the house of the dead man. Some claim that this house is the one now known as Jubilee Cottage. A sea wall protects the current village from landslip. A thatched cottage was formerly inhabited by the coastguard, who would have had one of the best vantage points to observe all the comings and goings around the bay.

Runswick Bay and the only sandy beach walk in the book

WALK 44

Whitby, Saltwick Bay, Robin Hood's Bay and Hawsker

Start/finish	Whitby Station, NZ 898 108
Distance	21km (13 miles)
Total ascent/descent	220m (720ft)
Time	6hrs 30mins
Terrain	A moderate walk where urban walking gives way to a cliff coast path with a series of short ascents and descents; the second half of the walk uses a firm, clear and easy railway trackbed through cultivated countryside
Maps	OS Landranger 94; OS Explorer OL27 North
Refreshments	Plenty of pubs, restaurants and cafés at Whitby and Robin Hood's Bay; pub and café at Saltwick Bay; pubs at Hawsker and Stainsacre
Transport	Regular Arriva buses link Whitby and Robin Hood's Bay with Scarborough, Guisborough and Middlesbrough

The cliff coast path from Whitby to Robin Hood's Bay is a classic short day's walk that could be accomplished in a morning or an afternoon, leaving plenty of time to explore the sights at either end. Regular bus services run between both places too. However, there is also an old railway trackbed that once linked Robin Hood's Bay and Whitby. This is now the Cinder Track, and it is available to walkers and cyclists. The trackbed is firm and clear throughout, rising and falling so gently that it might as well be level. Walkers who follow it pass an interesting station site at Stainsacre, and finish by crossing a towering brick viaduct high above the River Esk.

Start from the bus station or railway station in Whitby and walk along the harbour to reach the Swing Bridge, the lowest bridge in town. After crossing the bridge, turn left along a narrow cobbled street lined with a variety of shops. Climb the famous 199 stone steps to reach St Mary's Church. Caedmon's Cross stands at the top of the steps, just to the left. Either explore the churchyard and church, founded in the 12th century, or continue straight ahead towards **Whitby Abbey**. Next, either turn right to visit the abbey, or turn left to follow the road away from it. Turn left again along a tarmac path to reach a cliff-top path.

WHITBY ABBEY

St Hilda founded Whitby Abbey in AD657. According to legend, fossilised ammonites were said to be snakes that she turned to stone! The Danes destroyed the abbey in AD867 and another foundation of 1078 was also unsuccessful. Much of what is seen today dates from the 12th century. However, the original abbey was founded in time to host the Synod of Whitby in AD664. This was when the Celtic and Roman Christian traditions, separated during the Dark Ages in Europe, settled some of the differences that each had accrued over the years, and agreed a method for calculating the movable feast of Easter. The abbey is also famous for one of its early lay brothers, Caedmon, who was inspired to sing in a dream one night, and whose words are the earliest written English Christian verse. The abbey is managed by English Heritage and there is an entrance charge, tel 01947 603568.

The atmospheric cliff-top ruins of Whitby Abbey stand high above Whitby town

Follow the cliff path onwards to Saltwick Bay and enjoy the open coastal scenery. **Saltwick Nab** is a prominent humpbacked headland, but one that largely results from the quarrying of alum shales. There is access to the beach if required, otherwise walk along the road through the Whitby Holiday Village, where there is a campsite, shop, pub and café. Just as the road leaves the site, a Cleveland Way signpost points left along the grassy cliff path. There is a view down to the isolated sea stack of **Black Nab**, which was also formed by alum shale quarrying. ▸

The twisted wreckage of the Admiral Von Tromp, which ran aground in 1976, can be seen near the beach.

Pass from field to field using kissing gates, keep to the seaward side of a foghorn, but follow a path on the landward side of a lighthouse. Climb higher along the cliff path, to around 90m (295ft) above sea level. The path basically rolls along, rising and falling fairly gently, sometimes with short flights of steps, with rugged cliffs down to the left and fields rising to the right. The route also crosses a couple of steep-sided wooded valleys. At a point where a path heads inland to Hawsker, there is a bench and a small garden, but no habitation in view. The path goes down 30 steps and crosses a footbridge in a small wooded valley as it passes **Maw Wyke Hole**. Climbing from the valley, there is access inland to a café/bar on a caravan park. ▸ The path continues, crossing a couple of small, stone-slab footbridges, and later crosses a couple more footbridges as it crosses a gentle valley at Rain Dale. Enjoy views back along the cliff coast.

The celebrated Coast to Coast Walk joins here.

Walk around **Ness Point** to see Robin Hood's Bay, but only after passing below the old coastguard hut and entering the Rocket Post Field. The path runs to the top end of the village via Mount Pleasant North, where a decision must be made: either continue along the road and turn left to walk down past higgledy-piggledy houses at **Robin Hood's Bay**, or simply turn right uphill and right again, barely setting foot on tarmac, to follow an old railway trackbed straight back to Whitby. ▸

See Walk 45 for information about Robin Hood's Bay.

The old railway trackbed above Mount Pleasant North is known as the Cinder Track. Simply crunch the cinder surface underfoot to leave Robin Hood's Bay. The

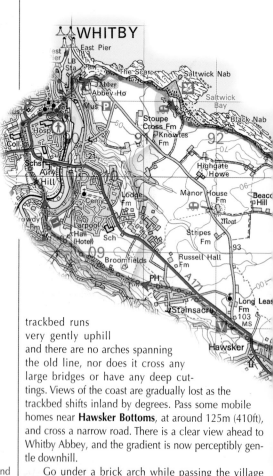

trackbed runs
very gently uphill
and there are no arches spanning
the old line, nor does it cross any
large bridges or have any deep cut-
tings. Views of the coast are gradually lost as the
trackbed shifts inland by degrees. Pass some mobile
homes near **Hawsker Bottoms**, at around 125m (410ft),
and cross a narrow road. There is a clear view ahead to
Whitby Abbey, and the gradient is now perceptibly gentle downhill.

*The Hare and
Hounds offers
food and drink
in the village.*

Go under a brick arch while passing the village
of **Hawsker**, and cross the busy **A171** using a pedes-
trian/equestrian crossing. ◄ Continuing along the old
trackbed, the path is narrower until it passes the old
railway station site just before **Stainsacre**, which now
operates as Trailways Cycle Hire, featuring a café, and

accommodation in a railway carriage. Later, cross a small iron bridge over a road and note the Windmill Inn to the right.

Walk alongside a woodland, then go gently down through a wooded cutting before gaining views towards Ruswarp and Eskdale on the left. Cross a monumental brick viaduct over the tidal River Esk and pass beneath three arches in a cutting that obscures views of **Whitby**. Pass beneath one final arch,

Robin Hood's Bay with the rugged cliffs of Ravenscar seen in the distance

223

then turn right down a flight of steps to reach a road. Walk down the road and go through a mini-roundabout as directed for the town centre. Note that the road passes Pannett Park, where there is an interesting museum, otherwise keep walking to return to the bus and railway stations.

CAPTAIN COOK

After moving to Whitby from Staithes in 1747, James Cook became an apprentice seaman, lodging in an attic belonging to his Quaker master John Walker. The apprentices learned the art of navigation and seamanship through lessons and hands-on experience on coal-carriers sailing to and from London. Cook's naval career began in 1755 and lasted for almost 25 years, until his untimely death in Hawaii in 1779. It is no doubt a testimony to Whitby's shipbuilding expertise that four of Captain Cook's ships were built in the town: *Endeavour, Resolution, Discovery* and *Adventure*. A replica of *Endeavour* can be found in the harbour, where it can be boarded and inspected, and it often sails out of the harbour for short trips. The Captain Cook Memorial Museum on Grape Lane charts the life and times of this remarkable explorer. There is an entrance charge, tel 01947 601900.

WHITBY

As a town Whitby developed greatly from the mid-18th to mid-19th centuries, when its fishing fleets turned to whaling. Whalers spent months at sea and did not always return with a catch. Whale blubber was highly prized, as the oil rendered from it burned to give a bright and fairly soot-free light. Women of the era would have had more than enough reason to curse their whalebone corsets, but the trade allowed the town to prosper immensely. A whalebone arch was erected above the town in 1853, replaced in 1963 by bones from Norway and replaced again in 2003 by bones from Alaska. Facilities in Whitby include all types of accommodation, including a youth hostel and nearby campsite. There are banks with ATMs, a post office, toilets, and an abundance of pubs, restaurants, cafés and takeaways. The tourist information centre is on Endeavour Wharf, tel 01723 383636.

WALK 45
Robin Hood's Bay, Boggle Hole and Ravenscar

Start/finish	Station House, Robin Hood's Bay, NZ 949 054
Distance	13.5km (8½ miles)
Total ascent/descent	270m (885ft)
Time	4hrs 15mins
Terrain	Easy cliff coast walking with a few short steep ascents and descents, followed by field paths and a good, firm, clear railway trackbed.
Maps	OS Landranger 94; OS Explorer OL27 North
Refreshments	Pubs, restaurants and cafés at Robin Hood's Bay; Raven Hall Hotel and café at Ravenscar; Fylingdales Inn off-route at Fylingthorpe
Transport	Regular Arriva buses link Robin Hood's Bay with Whitby and Scarborough; Scarborough & District buses run between Ravenscar and Scarborough

The low cliff coast around Robin Hood's Bay is cleft by steep-sided wooded valleys at Boggle Hole and Stoupe Beck, but these are not particularly difficult to cross, and the walk to the village of Ravenscar is easy enough. A splendid length of disused railway trackbed can be used further inland to return from Ravenscar to Robin Hood's Bay. The old line features quite noticeable gradients, although in effect the route might as well be level as far as walkers and cyclists are concerned. The line loops far inland to cross wooded valleys and pass through cuttings, finishing at an old station site.

Start at the top end of the village of Robin Hood's Bay, where there is a car park beside Station House on Station Road. Leave the car park and turn right at the Grosvenor Hotel. Walk down the B1447 to a roundabout beside the Victoria Hotel. Continue down a steep and narrow road, with over 100 steps winding past jumbled houses and cottages to reach the rocky shore at a stout sea wall that holds the village in place. ▶

The Bay Hotel bears a plaque marking the end of the Coast to Coast Walk.

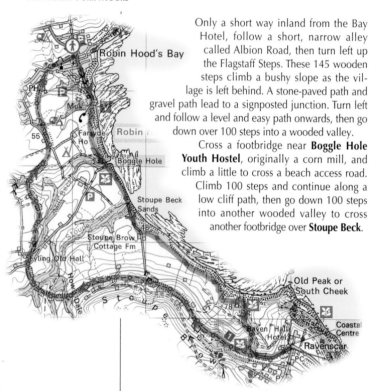

Only a short way inland from the Bay Hotel, follow a short, narrow alley called Albion Road, then turn left up the Flagstaff Steps. These 145 wooden steps climb a bushy slope as the village is left behind. A stone-paved path and gravel path lead to a signposted junction. Turn left and follow a level and easy path onwards, then go down over 100 steps into a wooded valley.

Cross a footbridge near **Boggle Hole Youth Hostel**, originally a corn mill, and climb a little to cross a beach access road. Climb 100 steps and continue along a low cliff path, then go down 100 steps into another wooded valley to cross another footbridge over **Stoupe Beck**.

Follow a narrow track, with 132 flagstone steps alongside, up a wooded slope to a car park. Pass Stoupe Bank Farm and follow its access road until you cross a slight dip. Turn left as signposted for the Cleveland Way, picking up the cliff path again. Views back along the coast reveal the little village of Robin Hood's Bay becoming distant, while ahead the village of Ravenscar draws nearer. The path is broad and grassy, running at around 60m (200ft) above sea level. It goes through small gates and crosses four footbridges – the last of which is flanked by dozens of steps – while heading inland.

Follow the path around the ruins of the Peak Alum Works as marked. Leave the site and turn left along a farm track made of concrete strips, and soon afterwards fork right up a clear path flanked by broom and gorse bushes. The path rises through woods and continues along a track studded with bricks that were made locally and stamped with the name . Walk to a road junction at the entrance gate of the **Raven Hall Country House Hotel**, near a visitor centre, at around 190m (625ft).

> The Romans built a signal station at **Ravenscar** more or less where the Raven Hall Hotel now stands. Alum mining was a profitable occupation in the area, leaving the cliffs around Old Peak looking rather bare. In the 1890s there was a grand scheme to create a tourist resort here, but despite a road system and drains being laid, very few investors bought plots or built properties, and the scheme ground to a halt in the 1920s. Ravenscar's history and heritage can be studied at the National Trust visitor centre, which incorporates a café.

Double back down the track from the visitor centre and step to the left on to the trackbed of an old railway line known as the Cinder Track. It passes under an arch and runs very gently downhill in a cutting, passing the old Brickyards Alum Quarry. Gorse and broom grow alongside the old line, which soon begins to drift further inland. Ewefield House stands close to the trackbed, on the right, while Browside Farm, on the left, is an attractive huddle of buildings. The old line reaches its furthest point inland in a well-wooded area where it crosses **How Dale** and strides high above Stoupe Beck. Pass a bridge with three arches where there is a glimpse of **Fyling Old Hall** to the left. Steps lead down on to a road, where a bridge has been demolished, and up the other side.

Keep right to continue along the old trackbed, passing the Station Master's House. Cross a minor road and pass Middlewood Farm Holiday Park, beyond which the trackbed becomes a tarmac path. Cross over a road between Fylingthorpe and Robin Hood's Bay and turn right to walk down the pavement beside the road for a short way. Fork left to walk parallel to the road as marked, passing Station House to return to the car park at **Robin Hood's Bay**.

ROBIN HOOD'S BAY

This charming and curiously complex village has a history of smuggling, where the villagers often engaged in hostilities with the revenue men. Local folk claim that a bolt of silk could be passed through secret cupboards and doorways, from the shore to the top of the village without seeing the light of day. They also tell of an incident when smugglers and revenue men waged a pitched battle in the bay, and it was possible to read newsprint at night from the flash of gunpowder. One thing seems certain: Robin Hood never had any association with the village. The Bay Hotel rises straight from the rocky fossil-rich shore – a hotel that over the years has seen one ship wrecked against its walls, as well as another poke its bowsprit straight through a window! The National Trust operates a visitor centre in the Old Coastguard Station opposite, tel 01947 885900.

The cascade of houses at Robin Hood's Bay is held in place by a stout sea wall

WALK 46

Cloughton, Staintondale, Ravenscar and Hayburn Wyke

Start/finish	Cloughton, TA 009 947
Distance	17.5km (11 miles)
Total ascent/descent	280m (920ft)
Time	5hrs 30mins
Terrain	The route follows an easy, firm and level railway trackbed for the first half of the walk; later it takes in a cliff coast path, which features a steep descent and ascent around Hayburn Wyke
Maps	OS Landrangers 94 and 101; OS Explorers OL27 South and OL27 North
Refreshments	Red Lion and Blacksmith's Arms at Cloughton; Raven Hall Hotel and cafés at Ravenscar; Hayburn Wyke Hotel at Hayburn Wyke
Transport	Regular Arriva buses link Cloughton with Scarborough and Whitby; Scarborough & District buses link Ravenscar with Cloughton and Scarborough

Throughout this walk an old railway trackbed runs parallel to the cliff coast between Cloughton and Ravenscar, and the distance between the old line and the cliff path is usually much less than 1km (½ mile). There are plenty of options to reduce the length of this walk simply by looking out for paths and tracks that cut across country from one half of the walk to the other. Anyone looking for a very short and scenic walk could turn off the line at the Hayburn Wyke Hotel and return quickly along the coast. The old line is known locally as the Cinder Track, while the cliff path is part of the Cleveland Way.

Leave the village of Cloughton by walking down Newlands Lane, passing renovated buildings at **Court Green Farm**. When you reach a bridge over an old railway trackbed, turn left to walk down on to the old line

The rugged and wooded slopes of Beast Cliff are protected as a nature reserve

There is easy access down to the beach at Hayburn Wyke for those who wish to shorten the route considerably.

and follow it onwards. The surface is level and cindery, and trees and bushes flank the line. Eventually, you will pass Northend House, which lies on the right, then the route runs through a well-wooded stretch. Go through a gate and cross a road, where the **Hayburn Wyke Hotel** is just down to the right, offering food, drink and accommodation. ◀

Continuing along the old line, note an old platform then go through another gate to walk further through woodlands. Pass beneath a stone arch and later cross a wooded valley on a curved embankment. Go under another stone arch and a gate that gives access to the former station at **Staintondale**, now a dwelling. The trackbed later crosses another wooded valley, then goes through two gates where a farm track crosses the line. There are more open views of the immediate country-side. Pass under another arch, and you will eventually reach the old railway platform at **Ravenscar**, close to a tearoom and a bus stop. The Raven Hall Country House Hotel is located along Station Road if a visit is required.

Simply head straight from the tearoom towards the cliffs and turn right to start following the coastal Cleveland

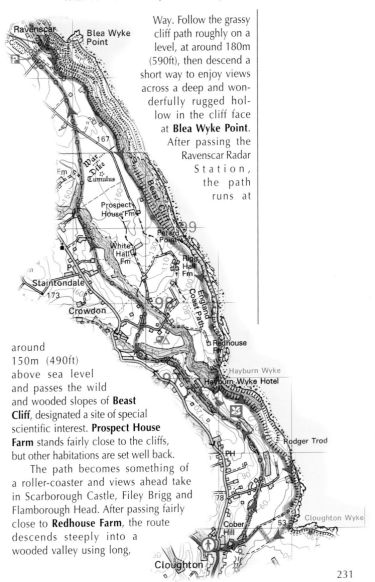

Way. Follow the grassy cliff path roughly on a level, at around 180m (590ft), then descend a short way to enjoy views across a deep and wonderfully rugged hollow in the cliff face at **Blea Wyke Point**. After passing the Ravenscar Radar Station, the path runs at

around 150m (490ft) above sea level and passes the wild and wooded slopes of **Beast Cliff**, designated a site of special scientific interest. **Prospect House Farm** stands fairly close to the cliffs, but other habitations are set well back.

The path becomes something of a roller-coaster and views ahead take in Scarborough Castle, Filey Brigg and Flamborough Head. After passing fairly close to **Redhouse Farm**, the route descends steeply into a wooded valley using long,

231

Cloughton Wyke is surrounded by cliffs rising from a bouldery beach

complex flights of wooden stairways and uneven stone steps. Cross two footbridges and consider a diversion down to the bouldery beach at **Hayburn Wyke**, where a small waterfall spills into a pool. Hayburn Wyke Hotel is located only a short way inland.

Climb lots of crude stone steps, then turn left. Walk up more stone steps on a slope covered with intriguingly twisted corkscrew oaks and rhododendron. Watch for a junction of paths and keep right, crossing another footbridge and moving further inland through the woods along the clearest path. Climb even further to leave the woods and continue along the top of the wooded slope, looking back towards the bay. When you reach a grassy crest at **Rodger Trod**, you will see a valley down to the right and the cliff coast to the left. Views ahead suggest a gentle descent, but the route is like a little roller-coaster.

Turn right just before reaching the head of **Cloughton Wyke**, following a route indicated by yellow arrows. A footpath leads inland and gently uphill alongside a field. Turn right alongside the field, then step left through a gap to continue straight to a minor road. Turn left and follow the road, which crosses a bridge over the old railway trackbed. Simply continue past **Court Green Farm** and follow Newlands Lane back into the village of **Cloughton**.

THE CINDER TRACK

The coastal railway between Scarborough and Whitby was engineered by John Waddell and ran from 1885. It brought places such as Robin Hood's Bay to the attention of tourists, but didn't seem to help plans for a resort at Ravenscar to get off the ground. The line was closed in 1965, but the trackbed remains open to walkers and cyclists as the Cinder Track, passing a handful of station sites and offering gentle gradients along the way. The full length of the line, along which it would be difficult to go astray, is about 30km (18½ miles) and most reasonably fit walkers could cover the distance in a day. Occasionally, hundreds of local schoolchildren use sections of the old railway line for sponsored walks. The old trackbed is part of the Sustrans National Cycle Route 1, but it is currently managed by Scarborough Borough Council.

A low and easy cliff line leads round the rugged little bay at Cloughton Wyke

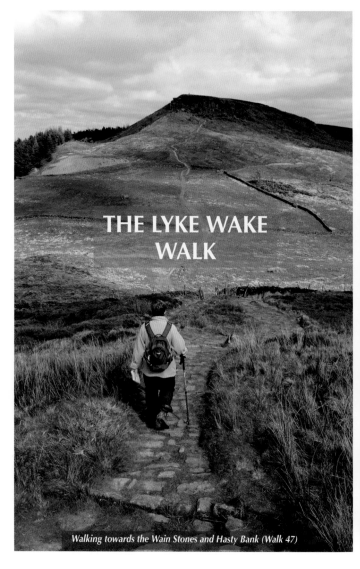

THE LYKE WAKE WALK

Walking towards the Wain Stones and Hasty Bank (Walk 47)

THE LYKE WAKE WALK

The Lyke Wake Walk was named after the Lyke Wake Dirge, a Yorkshire dialect verse describing the journey made across the dark and terrifying moors by a soul on its way to heaven or hell. There are several versions of the verse, which was already well established even in the 17th century, and it may well be the oldest known dialect verse in Yorkshire.

Credit where credit is due: the Lyke Wake Walk is one of the great classic walks, not only of the North York Moors, but of Britain. It was first mooted by local farmer Bill Cowley in 1955 and completed for the first time soon afterwards. Six decades of trail history cannot be condensed here, but countless thousands of walkers have risen (and fallen) to the challenge of walking some 65km (40 miles) across the moors within a strict 24-hour time limit. Tales of hardship, heroism, record breaking, success and failure have become the stuff of legends over the decades, and there is no doubt whatsoever that the route has been an inspiration and challenge to walkers.

Following the death of Bill Cowley the number of walkers completing the Lyke Wake Walk dwindled, and the club he founded for those who completed the route discussed whether they should disband, or continue. In fact, both things happened, with the 'old' club closing down and a 'new' club being founded, keeping the traditions of the walk alive, lykewake.org. However, maybe some walkers should look at the route anew. After decades of self-inflicted hardship, perhaps it is worth taking the time to appreciate the surroundings and enjoy the whole walk in daylight, rather than struggling through the hours of darkness on some godforsaken moorland grind. While most reasonably fit walkers could cover the distance over a tough weekend, the idea of taking four days over the route really does allow for a pleasant and leisurely walk.

Of course, taking four days means that additional distance will need to be covered in search of accommodation, since this is essentially a wild moorland route far from comfortable lodgings. In a couple of instances walkers might find it useful to time their arrival at certain roads in order to catch a bus to a nearby village for an overnight break. The first day's walk crosses the Cleveland Hills from Osmotherley to Clay Bank, where local accommodation providers will collect walkers and take them down to Chop Gate or Great Broughton.

The second day's walk leads over the High Moors from Clay Bank to Blakey Ridge, where the wonderfully remote Lion Inn offers accommodation. The third day's walk crosses another empty stretch of the High Moors, from Blakey to Eller Beck, where walkers should use Yorkshire Coastliner buses to reach villages

*View back across the moors traversed by
the Lyke Wake Walk near Ravenscar*

off-route. The fourth and final day's walk from Eller Beck leads over the Eastern
Moors to finish at Ravenscar, perched high above the Cleveland Coast.

Traditionalists may pour scorn on the notion of covering the Lyke Wake Walk
in stages, but the aim is to enjoy the route and its wilderness surroundings, rather
than suffer for the sake of meeting a deadline, walking through the night and
seeing little of the remarkable moorland scenery. Most walkers who enjoy a fine
day's walk will enjoy walking the Lyke Wake Walk in stages, and while they may
find each daily stretch a tough undertaking, many of them would be happy not to
increase their suffering fourfold!

WALK 47

Osmotherley, Carlton Bank, Cringle Moor and Hasty Bank

Start	Market Cross, Osmotherley, SE 456 972
Finish	B1257, Clay Bank, NZ 573 033
Distance	17.5km (11 miles)
Total ascent	800m (2625ft)
Total descent	700m (2295ft)
Time	5hrs 30mins
Terrain	A tough walk using a series of forest paths and hill paths, some of which are quite steep and rugged; the high moors are exposed
Maps	OS Landrangers 93 and 99; OS Explorer OL26 South and North
Refreshments	Queen Catherine Hotel, Golden Lion, restaurant and tearooms in Osmotherley; the Blacksmiths is off-route at Swainby; Lordstones Café at Carlton Bank
Transport	Regular Abbott's bus services to Osmotherley from Northallerton and Stokesley; summer weekend Moorsbus services cross Clay Bank

The first part of the Lyke Wake Walk is remarkably hilly, rather like a monstrous roller coaster running in tandem with the Cleveland Way and Coast to Coast Walk over the Cleveland Hills. Strong walkers could combine this day's walk with the following day's walk to Blakey, but the total distance and the effort involved would be daunting for some. Breaking the journey at Clay Bank involves descending to Great Broughton or Chop Gate in search of accommodation, although some providers offer pick-ups, returning walkers to the top of the road the following morning.

Leave the Market Cross in Osmotherley by following the road called North End. Pass a pinfold, where stray animals were once impounded. Turn left near the top of the village, as signposted for the Cleveland Way, along Ruebury Lane. Follow this access road as it climbs past a few houses, continuing uphill along a track to

237

reach a fork. Keep left to run close to **Chapel Wood Farm**, and keep straight ahead to walk away from it.

Go through a gate into **Arncliffe Wood**. Turn right up a clear path and continue along the inside edge of the wood, following a drystone wall over the crest of the hill. Pass the British Telecom station on Beacon Hill, as well as a trig point at 299m (981ft), then drop downhill to reach a couple of gates leading to heathery Scarth Wood Moor. A clear, paved path runs down the moorland slope, then a left turn leads down a steeper pitched path to reach a minor road at **Scarth Nick**.

A stone at this point commemorates Bill Cowley, who founded the classic Lyke Wake Walk.

Turn left down the road a short way to cross a cattle grid, finding a signpost pointing along a clear woodland path at **Coalmire**. Continue straight along a woodland track, then later turn left. ◀ Walk down a long flight of log steps. When you reach a gate at the bottom end of the wood, it offers access to the nearby village of

Swainby, if refreshments are required; otherwise, turn right without going through the gate to stay inside the wood, enjoying the sight of huge oak trees. Watch for a left turn later that leads out of the wood and down through a field. Follow a track to cross a footbridge or ford a river, then turn left to follow a road across a river in the wooded valley of Scugdale. Follow the road up to a road junction at **Huthwaite Green**.

The Cleveland Way is signposted from a gate, up a woodland path, passing ironstone spoil heaps where there are open views across the valley and plains. There is a sudden right turn up a steep, stone-pitched path on a wooded slope, then continue climbing less steeply up a stone-paved moorland path. This levels out as it crosses the 312m (1024ft) summit of **Live Moor**.

Cross a broad and heathery dip in the moorland, then climb again on **Holey Moor**, passing alongside a former gliding club field, now overgrown. You will reach a trig point at 408m (1338ft) alongside a stone upright on Carlton Moor. ▶ Follow a stone-paved path steeply down to a gap, passing close to a quarried edge protected by a fence. Cross a track and a road on the lower slopes of **Carlton Bank**.

Map continues on page 240

Enjoy splendid views across the plains, from the distant Pennines to industrial Teeside, past the little peak of Roseberry Topping, around the North York Moors and back towards Osmotherley.

A Lyke Wake Walk marker stone points the way towards the Cleveland Hills

Continue onwards, but note the immediate access to toilets and the Lordstones Café in a car park surrounded by trees. (Camping is available in the Country Park, but ask first at the café.) Walk across a grassy common to leave the café, then follow a grassy track, flanked by a fence and drystone wall, through a gate. Go through a gate and continue up a paved path close to the wall. You will reach a stone viewpoint seat dedicated to local rambler Alec Falconer at Cringle End. Climb higher along a gritty path and a paved path along the top of the abrupt northern edge of **Cringle Moor**, at around 420m (1380ft).

A steep, winding stone-pitched path leads downhill, passing shale spoil before reaching a fork at a gap. Keep right at the fork to go through a gate, then follow another steep, stone-pitched path over the top of **Cold Moor** at 401m (1316ft). Drop down to another gate and another grassy gap.

The next steep climb passes to the left of the jagged, blocky **Wain Stones**, which are worth studying from all angles and are completely out of character with the smooth contours prevalent around the North York Moors. Some hands-on scrambling is required, then once above them, a delightful level path runs along a moorland edge at 390m (1280ft) on **Hasty Bank**. At the end of this lofty promenade a steep path runs downhill, later following a wall. Some 60 stone steps complete the descent to the B1257 on **Clay Bank**.

Reaching the road on Clay Bank is not strictly the end of the day's walk. Strong walkers may well cross the road and continue onwards, while others will be happy to be collected, by prior arrangement, by accommodation providers from the two nearest villages of Great Broughton or Chop Gate. Walking off-route to these places adds another 4km (2.5 miles) to the day's walk, which might have to be repeated the following morning.

CHOP GATE AND GREAT BROUGHTON

The hamlet of Chop Gate is located down the road in Bilsdale, where facilities are limited to the Buck Inn, which offers food, drink and accommodation, including cabins and a campsite.

The village of Great Broughton is located down the road to the plains. The Wainstones Hotel offers food, drink and accommodation; the Bay Horse offers food and drink, and there are a couple of B&Bs in the area as well as a post office shop.

Looking back along the route to Beacon Hill from the crest of Live Moor

WALK 48

Clay Bank, Urra Moor, Bloworth Crossing and Blakey

Start	B1257, Clay Bank, NZ 573 033
Finish	Lion Inn, Blakey, SE 678 997
Distance	13.5km (8½ miles)
Total ascent	260m (855ft)
Total descent	120m (395ft)
Time	4hrs 30mins
Terrain	A moderate walk over high moors, mostly along good paths and tracks; the high moors are exposed
Maps	OS Landrangers 93 and 94; OS Explorer OL26 North and South
Refreshments	The Lion Inn at Blakey
Transport	Summer weekend Moorsbus services cross Clay Bank from the nearby villages of Great Broughton and Chop Gate; summer weekend Moorsbus services link the Lion Inn with Danby and Pickering

This is a lofty and remote part of the Lyke Wake Walk, traversing the highest part of the North York Moors and with no easy access to facilities of any kind. At the end of the day on Blakey Ridge, accommodation, food and drink are limited to the Lion Inn. Walkers who cannot secure lodgings and do not wish to cover any more of the route should check the summer weekend Moorsbus timetables to reach nearby towns and villages. Paths and tracks are generally clear, but a wrong turning at a junction could involve a huge detour. In clear weather this is one of the most memorable parts of the route, especially when the heather moorlands are flushed purple in the summer.

Leave the B1257 on **Clay Bank** and follow a steep, stone-pitched path uphill alongside a wall. Go through small gates, then at the top of the slope the path runs at an gentler gradient across the higher moorlands. The broad crest is called Carr Ridge and rises to around 380m (1250ft).

There are views back to the hilly parts of the Lyke Wake Walk, but now the terrain, although remote and exposed, is gentler. The path is mostly gritty, with grass, heather or bilberry alongside, although a few short stretches are paved with stone. Keep left, roughly along the crest of **Urra Moor**, until passing close to a trig point. This sits on a burial mound on **Round Hill** at 454m (1490ft) and can be reached by a short diversion along a path. ▸ Note the Hand Stone and Face Stone beside the track, which are ancient route markers across the moor.

It is the highest point on the moors, as well as in the whole of this guidebook!

The trig point on **Round Hill** sits on the squat remains of a moorland burial mound. The North York Moors are dotted with similar mounds, and some parts are criss-crossed by ancient earthworks that were either territorial markers or defensive structures. The moorland marker stones are of more recent antiquity, dating from around the 18th century. The Hand Stone has two open palms, bearing the words: 'this is the way to Stoxla' (Stokesley) and 'this is the way to Kirbie' (Kirkbymoorside). The older Face Stone features a crudely carved face.

Round Hill on Urra Moor is the highest point in the whole of the North York Moors

Continue along the clearest track and later pass a junction with another track, keeping straight ahead. When the track suddenly turns left, leave it by following a path on the right. This runs down a moorland slope and is partly stone-paved, climbing a short way to reach an old railway trackbed. Turn right to pass a barrier gate and reach a signposted intersection of tracks at **Bloworth Crossing**, at 388m (1273ft). The Cleveland Way turns left and is not seen again until Ravenscar, while the Lyke Wake Walk and Coast to Coast Walk run straight ahead.

Pass a barrier gate to walk along the trackbed of the former Rosedale

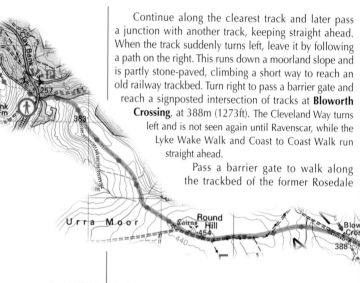

See Walk 30 and Walk 31 for historical notes about the old line.

Railway. ◄ First walk along a low embankment, then pass through a shallow cutting as the track curves left. Cross a moorland beck on a little embankment, then the cutting at **Middle Head**, which can be a bit wet and muddy. The track curves and crosses another little embankment across another moorland beck, and enjoys fine views over Farndale from **Dale Head**. Gentle curves give way to a long low embankment that slips over the moorland crest, so that you look down into Westerdale for a change. You will reach a junction with tracks that lead down into Farndale and over to Westerdale, but keep straight ahead.

The old railway trackbed rises very gently and overlooks Farndale again from Farndale Moor. On the way uphill there are more curves, then suddenly, as you reach a shallow cutting, you will see the Lion Inn on a moorland crest across a valley. The trackbed makes a great curve around the valley and the inn passes from sight, but a small outbuilding remains visible and a path on the left climbs towards it.

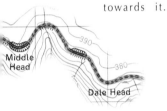

Keep to the left of the building, then turn right at the top of a drystone-walled enclosure. You will reach an old burial mound known as the Cockpit just before the **Lion Inn**.

Looking back along the stone-paved path from Carr Ridge across to Hasty Bank

BLAKEY

Blakey is a bleak spot, but food, drink and accommodation are offered at the celebrated Lion Inn, at over 400m (1315ft). The inn was once popular with the coal and ironstone miners who worked on the moors, and is popular today with walkers, bikers and motorists. Summer weekend Moorsbus services link the inn with Danby and Pickering. Walkers following the Lyke Wake Walk have only three options: stay at the Lion Inn, use the Moorsbus to reach other accommodation or keep walking.

WALK 49

Rosedale Head, Hamer, Wheeldale Moor and Simon Howe

Start	Lion Inn, Blakey, SE 678 997
Finish	Eller Beck Bridge, SE 858 982
Distance	21.5km (13½ miles)
Total ascent	200m (655ft)
Total descent	420m (1380ft)
Time	7hrs
Terrain	A tough walk over high moorlands but mostly on well-trodden paths, although some parts are rugged, boggy or vague; care is needed with route-finding in places; the high moors are exposed
Maps	OS Landranger 94; OS Explorers OL26 North, OL27 North and OL27 South
Refreshments	The Lion Inn at Blakey
Transport	Summer weekend Moorsbus services link the Lion Inn with Danby and Pickering; Yorkshire Coastliner buses pass Eller Beck Bridge, linking with Lockton, Pickering, Goathland and Whitby

This is a long and tough stage, where good weather helps enormously. The Lyke Wake Walk always stays on the high moors and pursues a direct course regardless of the nature of the terrain. Deeply worn paths can be muddy or stony underfoot, although sometimes the route can be a little vague too. Wheeldale Moor is particularly rough underfoot and should not be crossed in a hurry. Beyond Wheeldale the route across the broad moor of Simon Howe is relative easy. However, Eller Beck Bridge is in the middle of nowhere and walkers finishing at this point need to catch a bus elsewhere to find accommodation.

Leave the Lion Inn and walk along the road in the direction of Castleton. Watch for a bridleway signposted off to the right, where a trodden path crosses a dip in the moorlands at **Rosedale Head**, passing a couple of chunky boundary stones before rising back to a road. Have a look at the curious whitewashed marker stone of **White Cross**, known locally as Fat Betty. Turn right and follow the moorland road until you reach a junction with the Fryup road. Some walkers choose to avoid the road and walk in a straight line, linking a series of boundary stones with whitewashed tops. ▶

The Coast to Coast Walk turns left at the road junction and is not seen again.

Take note of a moorland marker, in the shape of a huge standing stone, planted at this junction by the North York Moors Authority in 2000. It serves to illustrate that the tradition of erecting stones on these bleak moors still lives! Follow the Rosedale road onwards a little, then turn left up the only clear path in sight. This path has been deeply eroded into a stony or peaty groove up the heather slopes of Seavey Hill, following a line of white-topped boundary stones. Cross a rise at **432m** (1417ft) and walk downhill to pass the larger Causeway Stone, where a flagstone causeway slices across the moorland. The Lyke Wake Walk is at first broad and eroded, then crosses a broad, sodden, rushy dip on the moor.

Climb gently up another slope beyond, then the gradients are barely perceptible across **Rosedale Moor**. The path remains broad and clear and is generally firm underfoot as it forges through the heather, at around 390m (1280ft). Cross the gentle valley of North Gill, where you

The Lyke Wake Walk crosses stepping stones over Wheeldale Beck

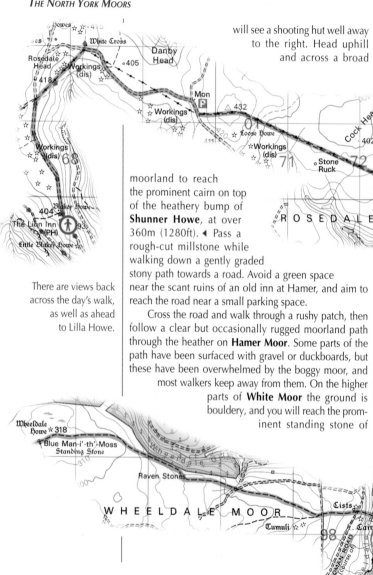

will see a shooting hut well away to the right. Head uphill and across a broad

moorland to reach the prominent cairn on top of the heathery bump of **Shunner Howe**, at over 360m (1280ft). ◄ Pass a rough-cut millstone while walking down a gently graded stony path towards a road. Avoid a green space near the scant ruins of an old inn at Hamer, and aim to reach the road near a small parking space.

Cross the road and walk through a rushy patch, then follow a clear but occasionally rugged moorland path through the heather on **Hamer Moor**. Some parts of the path have been surfaced with gravel or duckboards, but these have been overwhelmed by the boggy moor, and most walkers keep away from them. On the higher parts of **White Moor** the ground is bouldery, and you will reach the prominent standing stone of

There are views back across the day's walk, as well as ahead to Lilla Howe.

Blue Man-i'-th'-Moss. ▶ Nearby is the heathery hump of Wheeldale Howe at 318m (1043ft); the moorland supports a few conifers that appear to have escaped from a nearby plantation.

It was once painted blue, but now a 'blue man' has been painted on it.

Watch carefully to spot the line of a narrow path as it crosses very rough and bouldery moorland that has plenty of wet patches. The path narrows as it runs closer to the forest plantation, then drifts away from it and becomes broader. Keep following it and the terrain eases as **Wheeldale Moor**

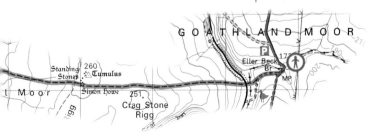

slopes gradually down to a minor road. Cross the road and a stile over a fence to continue downhill alongside a fence. Cross over the ancient 'Roman Road' and continue downhill, soon picking a way down a steep and bouldery slope covered in bracken. Stone steps lead to **Wheeldale Beck**, and stepping stones lead across to the other side. ▶

A prominent building nearby, Wheeldale Lodge, once served as a youth hostel.

Follow a path straight up another slope of bracken. Step across a track and walk up past a rocky brow to reach a cairn on Howl Moor, where heather moorland stretches ahead. Simply follow parallel paths, which are wet in places but fairly easy and obvious, up to a cairn on top of **Simon Howe**. There is a trig point off-route at 260m (853ft), but it doesn't have to be visited. Enjoy views around the higher moors, whose near-horizontal lines are broken only by the pyramid at RAF Fylingdales.

Keep walking straight ahead to descend gradually on the moorland slope. The path steepens a little, then be sure to watch and listen for trains while crossing the North Yorkshire Moors Railway line. A path made of railway sleepers crosses the Fen Bog Nature Reserve and leads uphill. Walk along a track to reach the busy A169 at **Eller Beck Bridge**.

Cairn on Simon Howe before the final descent to Eller Beck Bridge

Due to the nature of the road, which bends as it crosses the bridge, buses are obliged to slow down. This is a recognised Yorkshire Coastliner bus stop, but it is rarely used, and it is therefore necessary to give an obvious signal to the driver in good time. Note that the only places the bus can stop are where there are junctions with tracks on either side of the road. Buses can be used to leave the route in search of accommodation at nearby Goathland or further away at Lockton, Pickering or Whitby.

WALK 50

Eller Beck, Lilla Howe, Jugger
Howe Moor and Ravenscar

Start	Eller Beck Bridge, SE 858 982
Finish	Raven Hall Hotel, Ravenscar, NZ 980 017
Distance	13.75km (8½ miles)
Total ascent	260m (855ft)
Total descent	250m (820ft)
Time	4hrs 30mins
Terrain	A tough walk over high moorlands, but mostly along good paths and tracks; the high moors are exposed
Maps	OS Landranger 94; OS Explorer OL27 South and North
Refreshments	The Flask Inn lies well off-route on the A171; the Raven Hall Hotel and cafés are available at Ravenscar
Transport	Yorkshire Coastliner buses cross Eller Beck Bridge between Pickering and Whitby; regular Arriva buses link the Flask Inn with Whitby and Scarborough; Scarborough & District buses link Ravenscar with Scarborough

The last part of the Lyke Wake Walk traverses a broad moorland crowned by Lilla Cross. Views back along the route and ahead reveal how astonishingly direct the route really is. Walkers cross the rugged valley, drained by Jugger Howe Beck, to continue, then climb gently over one last moor to gain a view of their ultimate destination – Ravenscar. Over the past decades most Lyke Wake Walk participants have been content to limp down the road to finish, but with more time at your disposal, paths and tracks can be linked to complete the walk at a leisurely pace, and still leave time to explore the village.

Walkers reaching Eller Beck Bridge by bus should give the driver plenty of notice that they want to get off. The road bends as it crosses the bridge, and while this is a recognised Yorkshire Coastliner bus stop, it is awkward. Leave the busy A169 road and follow a track that is

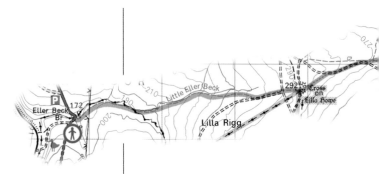

Some walkers follow the posts and a wet and muddy path has formed as a result.

Although of no great height, this moorland top offers extensive views through the heart of the North York Moors.

clearly marked as running on to MOD property – part of RAF Fylingdales. Go through a gate and walk beneath a pylon line to the end of the track. Keep to the left-hand side of a fence to continue, following a path across a boggy area full of bog myrtle. The path aligns itself to **Little Eller Beck** and pulls away from the fence. A line of metal posts have been planted all the way up the heather moorland slope, and the idea is always to keep well to the left of them. ◀ It can be muddy underfoot in places, but later you will reach a firm gravel track and a left turn leads to a gate. Go through the gate and cross another track, walking straight ahead up a more rugged path on a heathery slope. Cross a rugged track, then aim for the **cross on Lilla Howe**, at 292m (958ft). ◀

Walk straight ahead down a path from Lilla Howe, keeping right along a track to reach a track junction where there is a boulder. Branch left along a track that can be rough and stony as well as muddy when wet. It is clear and obvious as it descends

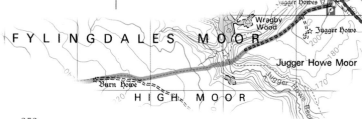

gently over Fylingdales Moor, passing a cairn on a mound known as **Burn Howe**. The track becomes a narrow path, but remains clear to follow, becoming steep and stone-paved as it drops towards **Jugger Howe Beck**.

Cross a footbridge over the beck and turn right. Follow a path uphill among bracken and heather on **Jugger Howe Moor**. Walk along a clear track that becomes a concrete road leading to a gate. Cross a road that was formerly the main road, then cross the rather busy A171 with care. ▸

The route climbs straight up the road cutting, then follows a narrow path across **Stony Marl Moor**. The moorland is heathery and dotted with trees. As you gain height, a clear track forms and leads close to a minor road beside a tall communication mast. The height at this point is 266m (873ft), and there are no more hills to climb.

A left turn leads to the Flask Inn, which offers accommodation, food and drink. Buses also stop there, but won't stop on the main road over the moors.

Lilla Cross stands on Lilla Howe and offers wide ranging views across the moors

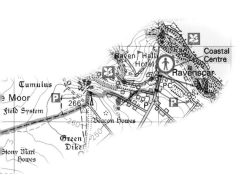

For the descent turn left along the road, then almost immediately branch right along a narrow path, or if this is overgrown, use a nearby track. This runs across the last little patch of heather moor on Stoupe Brow. Cross a step-stile on the right and walk down a rough grassy slope to reach another step-stile at the bottom. Turn right to follow a farm road, then turn left later down a farm access road as signposted public

Crossing Stony Marl Moor before the end of the route at Ravenscar

footpath. Leave it by walking down to the right, then at a junction of paths turn right up across a slope. Turn left to walk down the road towards the **Raven Hall Hotel** in **Ravenscar**, bringing this long walk across the moors to a close. There is a café at the National Trust visitor centre, as well as a tearoom at the end of Station Road.

CAUTIONARY TALE

Those who insist on covering the whole of the Lyke Wake Walk in 24 hours are reminded of a short conversation that took place a long time ago between a customer and a former proprietor in the café at Ravenscar:

'You must see some funny sights coming in here.'

'Yes, but they're funnier still when they try to get up to go out.'

APPENDIX A – ROUTE SUMMARY TABLE

Walk	Start	Distance	Total Ascent/Descent	Time	Page
The Tabular Hills					
Walk 1	West Ayton	15km (9½ miles)	240m (790ft)	5hrs	29
Walk 2	Hackness	9.5km (6 miles)	200m (655ft)	3hrs	34
Walk 3	Lockton	20km (12½ miles)	390m (1280ft)	6hrs	37
Walk 4	Levisham	10km (6¼ miles)	260m (855ft)	4hrs	43
Walk 5	Levisham Station	9.5km (6 miles)	260m (855ft)	3hrs	48
Walk 6	Hutton-le-Hole	15km (9½ miles)	260m (855ft)	5hrs	52
Walk 7	Gillamoor	8km (5 miles)	140m (460ft)	2hrs 30mins	57
Walk 8	Newgate Bank	17km (10½ miles)	230m (755ft)	5hrs 30mins	60
Walk 9	Helmsley	10.5km (6½ miles)	150m (490ft)	3hrs 15mins	64
Walk 10	Hawnby	7.5km (4½ miles)	330m (1080ft)	2hrs 30mins	68
The Hambleton Hills					
Walk 11	Rievaulx Abbey	10.75km (6¾ miles)	160m (525ft)	3hrs 30mins	74
Walk 12	Byland Abbey	7.5km (4½ miles)	200m (655ft)	2hrs 30mins	78
Walk 13	Sutton Bank	13.5km (8½ miles)	310m (1015ft)	4hrs 45mins	82
Walk 14	Osmotherley	18km (11 miles)	460m (1510ft)	6hrs	87

Walk	Start	Distance	Total Ascent/Descent	Time	Page
The Cleveland Hills					
Walk 15	Osmotherley	13km (8 miles) (9.5km (6 miles) without detours)	390m (1280ft)260m (855ft)	4hrs or 3hrs without detours	94
Walk 16	Chop Gate	15.5km (9½ miles)	540m (1770ft)	5hrs	98
Walk 17	Chop Gate	14km (8¾ miles)	540m (1770ft)	5hrs	102
Walk 18	Kildale	16.5km (10¼ miles) or 10.5km (6½ miles)	410m (1345ft)	5hrs 15mins or 3hrs 15mins	106
Walk 19	Kildale	15.5km (9½ miles)	430m (1410ft)	5hrs	110
The Northern Moors					
Walk 20	Great Ayton	10.5km (6½ miles)	430m (1410ft)	3hrs 30mins	115
Walk 21	Guisborough	13.5km (8½ miles)	310m (1015ft)	4hrs 15mins	119
Walk 22	Danby	14km (8¾ miles)	280m (920ft)	4hrs 30mins	123
Walk 23	Scaling Dam	13km (8 miles)	240m (790ft)	4hrs 30mins	127
The High Moors					
Walk 24	Chop Gate	20km (12½ miles) or 14.5km (9 miles) using Moorsbus	580m (1900ft)	6hrs 30mins or 4hrs 30mins	134
Walk 25	Chop Gate	17.5km (11 miles) or 13km (8 miles) using Moorsbus	500m (1640ft)	5hrs 30mins(4hrs)	139

Walk	Start	Distance	Total Ascent/Descent	Time	Page
Walk 26	Low Mill	13km (8 miles)	360m (1180ft)	4hrs 30mins	144
Walk 27	Church Houses	19.5km (12 miles)	320m (1050ft)	6hrs	148
Walk 28	Hutton-le-Hole	12.5km (7¾ miles)	250m (820ft)	4hrs	152
Walk 29	Rosedale	14km (8¾ miles)	350m (1150ft)	4hrs 30mins	156
Walk 30	Rosedale	17.5km (10½ miles)	330m (1080ft)	6hrs	159
Walk 31	Blakey	16.5km (10¼ miles)	Total Ascent: 70m (230ft) Total Descent: 310m (1015ft)	5hrs	163
Walk 32	Westerdale	14.5km (9 miles)	360m (1180ft)	5hrs	167
Walk 33	Danby	14.5km (9 miles +)	450m (1475ft)	5hrs	172
Walk 34	Lealholm	22km (13¾ miles)	500m (1640ft)	7hrs	176
Walk 35	Glaisdale	20km (12½ miles)	500m (1640ft)	6hrs 30mins	181
The Eastern Moors					
Walk 36	Goathland	14.5km (9 miles)	260m (855ft)	5hrs	188
Walk 37	Moorgates	7.5km (4¾ miles)	Total Ascent: 20m (65ft) Total Descent:130m (425ft)	2hrs 30mins	192
Walk 38	Goathland	6.5km (4 miles)	200m (655ft)	2hrs	196
Walk 39	Goathland	16km (10 miles)	240m (790ft)	5hrs 30mins	199
Walk 40	Chapel Farm	17km (10½ miles)	300m (985ft)	5hrs 30mins	203
Walk 41	Sleights	12.5km (7¾ miles)	270m (885ft)	4hrs	206

Walk	Start	Distance	Total Ascent/Descent	Time	Page
The Cleveland Coast					
Walk 42	Runswick Bay	11.5km (7 miles)	200m (655ft)	3hrs 30mins	211
Walk 43	Runswick Bay	12.5km (7¾ miles)	200m (655ft)	4hrs	215
Walk 44	Whitby	21km (13 miles)	220m (720ft)	6hrs 30mins	219
Walk 45	Robin Hood's Bay	13.5km (8½ miles)	270m (885ft)	4hrs 15mins	225
Walk 46	Cloughton	17.5km (11 miles)	280m (920ft)	5hrs 30mins	229
The Lyke Wake Walk					
Walk 47	Osmotherley	17.5km (11 miles)	Total Ascent: 800m (2625ft) Total Descent: 700m (2295ft)	5hrs 30mins	237
Walk 48	Clay Bank	13.5km (8½ miles)	Total Ascent: 260m (855ft) Total Descent: 120m (395ft)	4hrs 30mins	242
Walk 49	Blakey	21.5km (13½ miles)	Total Ascent: 200m (655ft) Total Descent: 420m (1380ft)	7hrs	246
Walk 50	Eller Beck Bridge	13.75km (8½ miles)	Total Ascent: 260m (855ft) Total Descent: 250m (820ft)	4hrs 30mins	251

APPENDIX B
Useful contacts

North York Moors National Park
North York Moors National Park
Authority
The Old Vicarage
Bondgate
Helmsley
North Yorkshire
YO62 5BP
tel 01439 772700
www.northyorkmoors.org.uk

Sutton Bank National Park Centre
tel 01845 597426.

The Moors National Park Centre
Danby
tel 01439 772737.

Tourist Information Centres
Tourist information is available throughout the North York Moors, from dedicated information centres to simple information points. The level of service offered varies from assistance with accommodation bookings and items for sale, to simply having a selection of leaflets covering local attractions and services.

Main tourist centres
Scarborough

Stephen Joseph Theatre
Westborough
tel 01723 383636
www.discoveryorkshirecoast.com

Whitby

Harbour Office
Endeavour Wharf
tel 01723 383636
www.discoveryorkshirecoast.com

Great Ayton

Discovery Centre
High Street
tel 01751 475183

Pickering

Trailblazer
Outdoors Market Place
tel 01751 475183

Information points
- Rosedale Abbey: Abbey Stores and Tea Rooms
- Goathland: Post Office
- Grosmont: Steaming Loco
- Staithes: Gateway Business Centre
- Osmotherley: Top Shop
- Hutton-le-Hole: Ryedale Folk Museum

Public Transport

Rail
National Rail Enquiries
tel 03457 484950
www.nationalrail.co.uk

Northern
www.northernrailway.co.uk

North Yorkshire Moors Railway
www.nymr.co.uk

Bus
National Express
www.nationalexpress.com

Moorsbus
www.moorsbus.org

Arriva
www.arrivabus.co.uk/north-east

Yorkshire Coastliner
www.yorkbus.co.uk

East Yorkshire Motor Services
www.eyms.co.uk

Abbotts
www.abbottscoaches.co.uk

Ryecat
www.ryedalect.org

Abbeys
Byland Abbey
tel 01347 868614

Rievaulx Abbey
tel 01439 798228

Mount Grace Priory
tel 01609 883494

Guisborough Priory
tel 01287 633801

Whitby Abbey
tel 01947 603568

Access Land
Open Access Contact Centre
tel 0300 0602091

Museums and Attractions
Ryedale Folk Museum
tel 01751 417367
www.ryedalefolkmuseum.co.uk

Helmsley Castle
tel 01439 770442

Duncombe Park
tel 01439 770213
www.duncombepark.com

National Centre for Birds of Prey
tel 0844 7422035
www.ncbp.co.uk

Captain Cook Memorial Museum
Whitby
tel 01947 601900

Old Coastguard Station Robin Hood's
Bay
tel 01947 885900

NOTES

NOTES

NOTES

NOTES

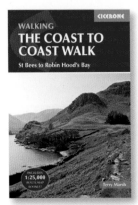
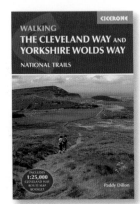
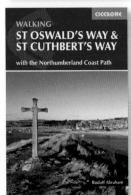
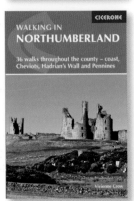

DOWNLOAD THE ROUTES
IN GPX FORMAT

All the routes in this guide are available for download from:

www.cicerone.co.uk/951/GPX

as GPX files. You should be able to load them into most formats of mobile device, whether GPS or smartphone.

When you go to this link, you will be asked for your email address and where you purchased the guide, and have the option to subscribe to the Cicerone e-newsletter.

www.cicerone.co.uk

LISTING OF CICERONE GUIDES

For full information on all our
guides, books and eBooks,
visit our website:
www.cicerone.co.uk

Walking – Trekking – Mountaineering – Climbing – Cycling

Over 40 years, Cicerone have built up an outstanding collection of over 300 guides, inspiring all sorts of amazing adventures.

Every guide comes from extensive exploration and research by our expert authors, all with a passion for their subjects. They are frequently praised, endorsed and used by clubs, instructors and outdoor organisations.

All our titles can now be bought as **e-books**, **ePubs** and **Kindle** files and we also have an online magazine – **Cicerone Extra** – with features to help cyclists, climbers, walkers and trekkers choose their next adventure, at home or abroad.

Our website shows any **new information** we've had in since a book was published. Please do let us know if you find anything has changed, so that we can publish the latest details. On our **website** you'll also find great ideas and lots of detailed information about what's inside every guide and you can buy **individual routes** from many of them online.

It's easy to keep in touch with what's going on at Cicerone by getting our monthly **free e-newsletter**, which is full of offers, competitions, up-to-date information and topical articles. You can subscribe on our home page and also follow us on **Facebook** and **Twitter** or dip into our **blog**.

Cicerone – the very best guides for exploring the world.

CICERONE

Juniper House, Murley Moss, Oxenholme Road, Kendal, Cumbria LA9 7RL
Tel: 015395 62069 info@cicerone.co.uk
www.cicerone.co.uk